Menander I Soter
the Bactrian Greek King
Emperor of India 163 –130 BCE

Screenplay by M. Tony Malliaras.

Tony Malliaras is an Honours in Musicology graduate from the University of

Melbourne. He was born in Melbourne, Victoria, Australia where he resides and does most of his writing in leafy Melbourne city. He divides his time between a career in Financial Services and progressing towards a specialization in Superannuation.

Tony receives inspiration for most of his writing from his overseas travel. His father George Malliaras, a successful accountant, inspired him by taking him to visit ancient Greek temples in Athens, Delphi and Pella in Greece. Trips to modern Turkey to visit the old capital of the Byzantine Empire and biographies of the Byzantine Emperors provided further stimulation for ideas. Trips to India on many occasions, and visiting the Golden Temple in Amritsar, the Red Fort in Delhi, the Taj Mahal in Agra, and the Pink Palace in Rajasthan, which also provide food for thought in his writing style. He also enjoys cooking Indian cuisine and conversing with the governor of the Punjab on the Shatabdi Express which also provided stimulation for his ideas.

His published works include:

1. *Alexander's Dream, Menander's Reality, the Impact of Hellenism on Ancient India*, Melbourne: Kindle Direct Publishing, 1998, 2015.
2. *Vaios Malliaras: A Paradigm for the Transmission of Hellenic Culture 1907-1988:* Melbourne: Kindle Direct Publishing, 2017.
3. *Vaios Malliaras 1907-1988: The Formation of a Folk Clarinettist in the Changing Landscape of Inter-War Greece 1918-1954*, Melbourne: Kindle Direct Publishing, 2017.
4. *Oral Tradition as Living Traditions in Greek Poetics,* Melbourne: Kindle Direct Publishing, 2017.

Screenplays:

1. *Alexander the Great,* Melbourne: Kindle Direct Publishing, 1996, 2018.
2. *Menander 1 Soter: The Bactrian Greek King: Emperor of India 163-130 BCE.* Melbourne: Kindle Direct Publishing, 2018.

Menander I Soter

Copyright Tony Malliaras.

All Rights Reserved, 2018.

Office: Pindar Productions Pty Ltd	Cover Design
M. Tony Malliaras	Carl Fromigoni, I.T.
7 Royston Avenue	PlannerWeb
Malvern E. VIC. 3145	408 / 89 High St.
Australia.	Kew, Vic. 3101
M: 0421945585	Australia.
E: tonymalliaras@yahoo.com	

Cast of Characters

1. Indian villagers, Hindu Priests, extras.
2. Shri G. R. Sharma, Indian Archaeologist.
3. Greek Tourist.
4. Local Hindu Priest.
5. Emperor Brihadathra of the Mauryan Empire of India.
6. General Pushyamitra Sunga I. Usurper who assassinates Emperor Brihadathra and assumes the throne of Magadha and persecutes and eliminates Buddhist Schools.
7. Four Royal Women Bodyguards of the Mauryan Emperor Pushyamitra of Greek origin.
8. Chief Ministers of the Partisan Party belonging to the assassinated Emperor Brihadathra who oppose General Pushyamitra Sunga.
9. Chief Minister Yajnasena of Vidarbha who opposes General Pushyamitra.
10. Narrator's Voice.
11. Menander I Soter. A Greek King of Bactria in north-eastern India. Supporter of the Buddhist Order and its ultimate champion.
12. Injured Woman.
13. Injured Monk.
14. Bactrian Greek troops / Indo-Greek troops whose allegiance is to General Menander.
15. Venerable Nagasena. A Leading Buddhist Monk who becomes Menander's friend.
16. Citizens of Sakala.
17. Yoga practitioners in Sakala city parks.
18. Royal Courier of King Menander.
19. Alexander the Great who conquers eastern India and departs 325 BCE.
20. Emperor Chandragupta who unites India in 310-305 BCE.
21. Demetrius II, King of Bactria and father of Menander of the House of Diodotus.
22. Apollodotus I of the House of the Euthydemids who rule Eastern Punjab, India.
23. Agathocles of the House of the Euthydemids who rule Eastern Punjab, India.
24. Pantaleon of the House of the Euthydemids who rule Eastern Punjab, India.
25. Davakos a Greek Champion Wrestler.

26. Bala an Indian Champion Wrestler.
27. Crowd in Arena: Extras.
28. Princess Agathocleia, daughter of Demetrius I who becomes the wife of Menander.
29. Devamantiya: Chief Advisor to General / King Menander of Bactria.
30. Anantakaya: Chief Advisor of General / King Menander of Bactria.
31. Makura: Chief Advisor of General / King Menander of Bactria.
32. Sabbadina: Chief Advisor of General / King Menander of Bactria.
33. Alexander: A Wealthy Greek Merchant who belongs to a power elite who control the known world's trade routes and influence kingdoms and regimes.
34. Court Officers: Menander's Royal Court.
35. Courier for Alexander, the mysterious and powerful Greek Merchant.
36. Casseiopiea of Nautika city. The real mother of the twin girls aged two.
37. Clyminestra of Nautika city. The false mother of the twin girls aged two.
38. Excurgus the Council Leader of 500 Councillors in Menander's Kingdom.
39. Crown Prince Agnimitra. Son of Emperor Pushyamitra Sunga of Magadha.
40. Prince Vasumitra. Son of Emperor Pushyamitra Sunga of Magadha.
41. Menander's Bactrian Cavalry: Extras.
42. Menander's Infantry: Extras.
43. Eucratides the rebel leader and ruler of the House of Eucratides of Western Punjab.
44. Emperor Pushyamitra's Secret Security Force. Extras.
45. Emperor Pushyamitra's Agents. Extras.
46. The Shop Keeper in the capital Pataliputra of the Mauryan Empire.
47. Emperor Pushyamitra's Advisers: Extras.
48. Emperor Pushyamitra's Chief Military Adviser.
49. Buddhist Monks persecuted by the Brahmin Faction of the Emperor Pushyamitra.
50. The Brahmin Faction who carry out a campaign of violence and terror on Buddhists.
51. The Venerable Elder of the Monastery of Kukkutarama.
52. European women in the Palace of Pleasures of Crown Prince Agnimitra.
53. Local Merchant in Chirand city, east of the Ganges Valley.
54. Two local champion wrestlers in Buxar city, in the Ganges Valley.
55. The Emperor's Agents in Buxar city.
56. The Venerable Elder of Ayodhya city in the Ganges Valley.
57. Ashoka, half Greek and half Indian, the greatest Emperor of India.

58. Menander's Chief Engineer.
59. Kirtana and Musicians in Sohgaura city, east of the Ganges Valley.
60. A Buddhist Emissary in Sohgaura city.
61. Bhikkhu Bodhi. In alliance with Menander.
62. Menander' Spymaster.
63. A Buddhist Monk of Ahichhatra city, north of the Ganges Valley.
64. The Emperor's troops.
65. A Buddhist Monk, north-west of the Ganges Valley.
66. A Kirtana performance with singers and musicians in Mathura city. Krishna's city.
67. Menander's Council of 500 Members.
68. Menander's Sub-King Agathocles.
69. A Greek guard.
70. Menander's Sub-King Pantaleon.
71. Gora Kalla. A spy for the Emperor Pushyamitra.
72. Lead Singer of the Kirtan Performance in Mathura city, north-west of the capital.
73. Vishnu, an ally of the Emperor Pushyamitra in Mathura city.
74. A Buddhist Monk of Mathura city.
75. The Festival of Diwali or Festival of Lights in Mathura city. Extras.
76. Chief Minister Yajnasena, Leader of the Partisan Party which opposes the Emperor.
77. Chief Minister of Kausambi city.
78. Chief Minister of Mathura city.
79. Chief Minister of Ahicchatra city.
80. A Priestess of the Cult of Anaitis, Goddess of Fertility, Bactria.
81. Andronicus a Greek Merchant in Mumbai, (Bombay) the caves of Nasik and Karli.
82. Athina, a Greek Merchant in Mumbai.
83. 50 Rajahs celebrate the Emperor Pushyamitra's Silver Jubilee or 25 years on the throne of Magadha.
84. The Royal Page who makes announcements for the Emperor of Magadha.
85. A Greek Merchant from Barygaza port city, in central-west India.
86. Second Greek Merchant of Barygaza port city.
87. Elite Group of Greek and International Merchants meet in Barygaza port city.
88. A Local Business Owner. Vishnu of Barygaza port city.
89. Hindu Religious Police in Delhi city.
90. A local farmer.

91. The farmer's daughter.
92. A friendly Buddhist Monk.
93. Vishnu, a local business owner in Barygaza port city.
94. First Guard who provides security for the power elite of Greek and International Merchants Meeting.
95. Andronicus a Greek Merchant.
96. Athina a Greek Merchant.
97. Unit Commander for Crown Prince Agnimitra.
98. Menander's Sub-King Epander.
99. Menander's Sub-King Polyxenus.
100. A Greek Naval Officer.
101. Indian forces loyal to the Emperor attack the Indo-Greek Naval Ships.
102. An Advance Scout for the Emperor.
103. The King of Mathura.
104. The King of Panchala.
105. Menander's Infantry; Cavalry; Engineering Units; Catapult Artillery Operators;
    Battery Ramp Operators; and Cretan Archers.
106. False Buddhist Monks.
107. Freed Buddhist Monks who celebrate their liberty from persecution.

APRIL-, 1979. AN ARCHAEOLOGICAL FIND IS MADE IN REN, ON THE LEFT BANK
OF THE YAMUNA RIVER, 96 KLM WEST OF KAUSAMBI, 350 KLM EAST OF
MATHURA, IN DISTRICT FATELPUR OF UTTAR PRADESH, INDIA.

Indian villagers and local Hindu priests carry a stone in ancient Mauryan script to the centre of their village and place it in their temple and begin to worship the stone.

>Local Merchant:
>Shri G. R. Sharma, the villagers have found a stone inscription in ancient Mauryan characters and have started worshipping it.

>Shri. G.R. Sharma:
>Take me to Ren.

They drive through dense forest and winding muddy roads to the site on the west bank of the Yamuna River. Sharma gets out of the car and walks up to the temple, where the stone inscription is held. He asks permission from the local priests to take a photo of it and is granted permission to do so. Sharma studies the 2.5 metre, tall stone and the ancient Mauryan characters on it. He scribbles the following in his note pad.

>*maharajasa rajarajasa*
>*mahamtasa tratarasa dhammi*

> *kasa jayamtasa ca apra*
> *jitasa Minanada de rasa.*

A local Greek tourist asks Sharma what it says. Shri G. R. Sharma, a scholar who is also a biased towards Greek rulers in India, reluctantly makes a transliteration.

> **Shri G. R. Sharma:**
> In Greek it reads:
> *BASILEOS BASILEON*
> *MEGALOU SOTEROS*
> *DIKAIOU NIKETOROU KAI ANIKETOU*
> *MENANDROU*

The local Greek tourists jumps for joy.

> **Local Greek Tourist:**
> That's Menander the King of Bactria,
> who conquered more Indian territories
> than Alexander the Great.

The Greek tourist begins to dance a merry dance around the Indian scholar, who holds his head, shaking it.

> **Shri G. R. Sharma:**
> Do you have any idea how many cities'
> Menander destroyed, including the capital
> of the Mauryan Empire, Pataliputra.

11

The Greek tourist stops dancing and approaches the Indian scholar.

                Local Greek Tourist:
                Was the Emperor of India, a tyrant at the time?

Both men look at the burnt conflagration of clay, stretching a hundred metres along the bank of the Yamuna River.

187 BCE. ASSASSINATION OF BRIHADATHRA, LAST EMPEROR OF MAGADHA.

PATALIPUTRA, CAPITAL OF THE MAURYAN EMPIRE.

General Pushyamitra rides his chariot into the capital of the Mauryan Empire, Pataliputra to bring a "letter" from the Bactrian Greek King Demetrius for the Emperor Brihadathra. He enters the opulent and splendour of the Magadhan Court. On the tall wall, 156 Indian Kings are depicted on the wall. Emperor Brihadathra has just attended a military parade.

>Emperor Brihadathra:
>General Pushyamitra, what letter do you bring
>from King Demetrius the Bactrian Greek?

General Pushyamitra looks left and right and sees that his fellow conspirators have evacuated the Royal Court. He walks up to the Emperor and whispers in his ear, asking his 12 Royal Bodyguards comprising Greek Women, to ward off any conspiracies in the Royal Mauryan Court, to leave as he has confidential information for the Emperor alone.

>General Pushyamitra:
>Leave us.

General Pushyamitra hands the letter to the Emperor who begins to read it closely. General Pushyamitra draws his sword and runs the Emperor Brihadathra through his back.

The Emperor looks up at his assassin, general Pushyamitra., who walks before the wall depicting 156 Indian Kings, raising his sword.

> General Pushyamitra:
> I Pushyamitra Sunga, am the new Emperor of India.

Emperor Brihadathra, with his dying breath, looks up at general Pushyamitra and utters the words.

> Emperor Brihadathra:
> Usurper, you shall die at the hands of the Greeks (Yavanas).

184 BCE. CHIEF MINISTERS LOYAL TO THE ASSASINATED EMPEROR BRIHADATHRA. A RIVAL FACTION TO THE NEW EMPEOR PUSHYAMITRA.

Yajnasena, Chief Minister of Vidarbha: Fellow Ministers of our beloved departed Emperor Brihadathra. General Pushyamitra has assassinated our leader, the last Emperor of the Mauryan Empire of India. A tyrant sits on the throne. Pushyamitra seeks to destroy the great work of our greatest leader, Emperor Ashoka, who promoted the ethics and morals of the Compassionate Buddha. He seeks to destroy the entire infrastructure of the Buddhist Order throughout India. He is secretly supporting a rival Brahminic Faction to seek and destroy Buddhist monasteries and Buddhist leaders throughout India. The new Emperor is too powerful for us to remove him. Pushyamitra has bought the loyalty of most of the governors, superintendents of cities and controls the main rivers in India. The Ganges, Jumna, Arciravati, Sarabhu and Mahi. There is only one man who can remove this tyrant from the throne. That man is general Menander, the Bactrian Greek. A foreigner. I know, I know, no foreign intervention. Just keep this option in mind. The fate of India is in your hands.

Ministers shake their heads negatively to approaching Menander a Greek general to remove an Indian Emperor. The Chief Ministers senses this and bides his time.

MAP OF ANCIENT INDIA

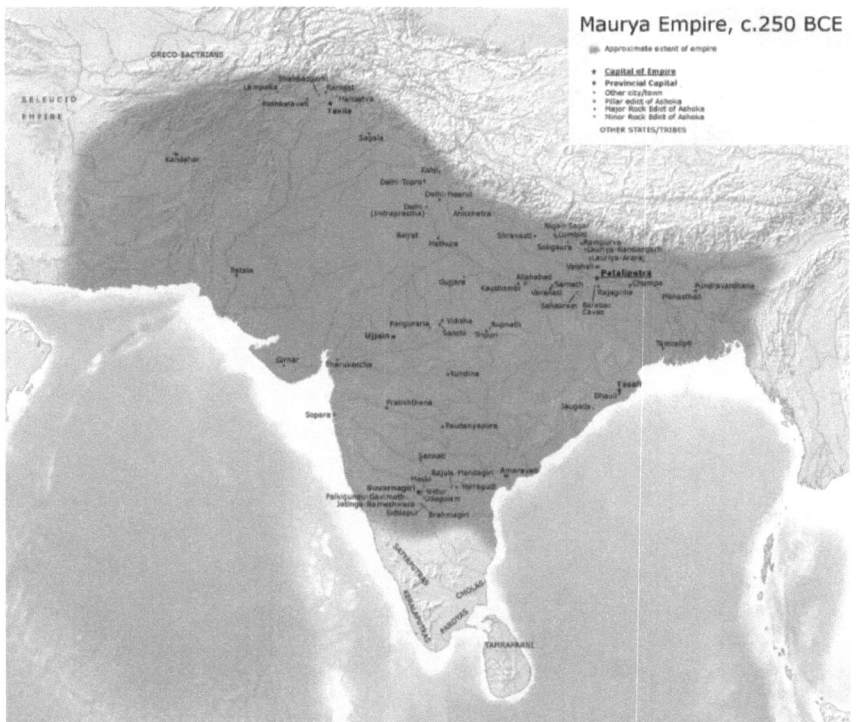

(Source: *Map of Ancient India, The Mauryan Empire*, By Avantiputra - Own work, CC BY-SA 3.0, https://commons.wikimedia.org/w/index.php?curid=33726301). Accessed 18/03/2018. See: Brian M. Fagan, *People of the Earth, An Introduction to World Prehistory,* Santa Barbara, University of California Press, 1998: 448. (*Map of the Mauryan Empire*: 449).

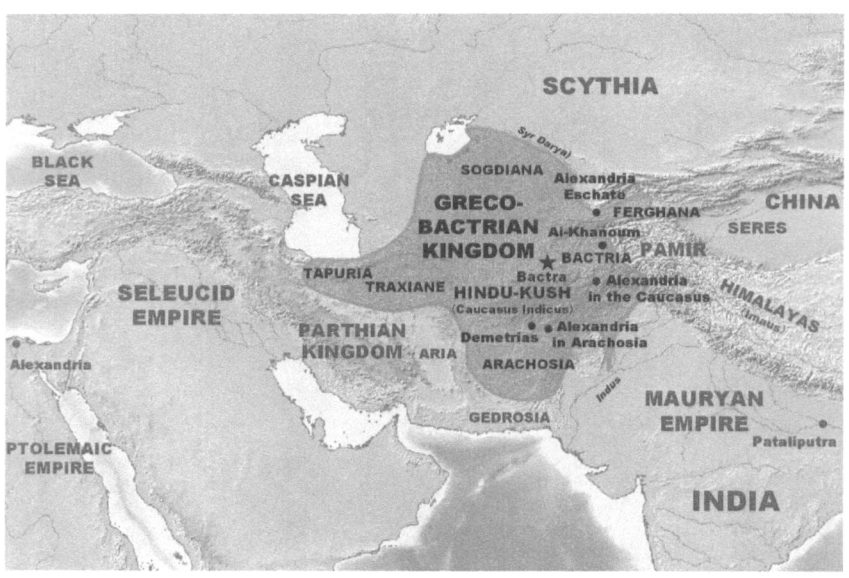

(Source: *Greco-Bactrian Kingdom 160 BCE*, Ancient History Encyclopedia, URL: www.googlemaps.com/Map of the Greco-Bactrian Kingdom. Accessed 10/04/2018).

(Source: *Greco-Bactrian Kingdom 160 BCE*, Ancient History Encyclopedia, URL: www.googlemaps.com/Map of the Greco-Bactrian Kingdom. Accessed 10/04/2018).

Narrator:

Alexander the Great left Punjab, India in 325 BCE. Chandragupta 1 ascended the Mauryan throne in 321 and a decade later, wiped out the Macedonian garrisons of northern India with an army of 600,000. Menander I descended from Greeks in Bactria, the dominion founded by Alexander, in present day Afghanistan. The Bactrian King Demetrius 189 – 167 BCE assumed power just when the Mauryan Empire was on the verge of collapse. Demetrius decides to exploit this situation to his advantage, and in a successful military campaign takes possession of Gandhara, the Punjab and the Indus Valley, establishing his capital in Taxila. Demetrius focusses on his military conquests and entrusts the administration of his states to his viceroys, chosen from the ranks of his own family. By 180 BCE. the Bacrtrians are in full possession of the eastern Punjab and Avanti and even threaten the Mauryan capital Pataliputra. Two rival kingdoms arise in the power struggle for the Bactrian Empire. The House of Eucratides or Western Greek Kingdom, comprises Bactria proper. The House of the Euthydemids, the Eastern Greek Kingdom comprising the Punjab, Gandhara and Kapisa. Menander assumes the throne upon the death of the first eastern ruler,

20

Apollodotus I 167 – 163 BCE. Emperor Pushyamitra Sunga supports the Brahmin faction. Menander supports the Buddhist Order in India. This is the story of how Menander I Soter realized Alexander's dream of conquering the capital of the Mauryan Empire, Pataliputra and liberated the Buddhists from the persecution of the Emperor of India.

175 – 163 BCE. MENANDER'S RISE TO POWER.

The sound of long bronze Buddhist horns and drums signals Menander's army returning from defeating his rival Eucratides in western Punjab, India. His army accidently destroys a Buddhist compound and a woman begins to scream and cry in pain as her leg is broken by passing horses and the wall of the compound collapsing around her. Inside the Buddhist compound, a monk continues to sit in meditation, unmindful of the commotion outside. Menander I Soter stops his horse and turns around to inspect the damage done by his cavalry.

> Menander I Soter:
> I am Menander, General of Demetrius, king of
> Bactria. Tell me who caused the wall to collapse on
> you?

The woman wipes the tears from her face and points to the general's soldiers.

> Injured Woman:
> O Great General, your troops caused the wall
> to collapse and injure me and the Buddhist
> monk.

The Buddhist monk, bleeding from bricks which crashed on his head, continues to sit in meditation. Menander inspects the damage once more. He turns to his doctor.

Menander I Soter:
Doctor dress the wounds of the monk.
My Bactrian Greeks, you shall rebuild
all damaged Buddhist monasteries in
Bactria, during your leave. I want this
compound rebuilt now.

Bactrian Greek troops flock around the compound and with speed and great focus rebuild theBuddhist compound. Venerable Elder Nagasena, visiting from a remote north-eastern corner of the Himalayas inspects the renovation. Menander I Soter, notices him.

Menander I Soter:
Venerable Elder, I am responsible for the damage
to your compound. I invite you to my palace in
Sakala. I wish to learn more about Buddhism.

Venerable Elder Nagasena:
General Menander, I am Nagasena, a humble servant
of the Buddha. I accept. I am also descended from
Greeks.

Narrator:
Menander lowers his head to the Venerable Elder
Nagasena and departs for his capital, Sakala, with his

army.

Menander enters Sakala, modern Sialkot to the cheers of his bi-lingual Bactrian Greek and Indian population. Behind him, ride on white horses, his four closest advisers. They are, Devamantiya, Anantakaya, Makura and Sabbadina.

Narrator:
In the *Milindapanha*, the wonders of Menander's capital Sakala are extolled. He states: There is in the country of The Yonakas (Greeks near Sialkot, in the hills of Jammu) a great centre of trade, a city which is called Sakala, situated in a delightful country well-watered and hilly, abounding in parks, gardens, groves and lakes and tanks, a paradise of rivers and mountains and woods. Wise architects have laid it out, and its people know of no oppression, since all their enemies and adversaries have been put down. Brave is its defence, with many and various strong towers and ramparts, with superb gates and entrance archways, and with the royal citadel in its midst, white-walled and deeply moated. Well laid out are its streets, squares, cross-roads and market-places. Well displayed are the innumerable sorts of costly merchandise with which its shops are filled. It is richly

adorned with hundreds of alms-halls of various kinds, and splendid with hundreds of magnificent mansions, which rise aloft like the mountain peaks of the Himalayas. Its streets are filled with elephants, horses, carriages and foot passengers, and crowded by men of all sorts and conditions – Brahmins, nobles, artificers, and servants. They resound with cries of welcome to the teachers of every creed, and the city is the resort of the leading men of each of the different sects. Shops are there for the sale of Benares muslin, of Kotumbar silks, and of other cloths of various kinds; and sweet odours are exhaled from the bazaars, where all sorts of flowers and perfumes are tastefully set out. Jewels are there in plenty, and guilds of traders in all sorts of finery display their goods in the bazaars that face all quarters of the sky.

Narrator:
Life in Sakala is wondrous. The granaries are always full of corn. Gold, silver and copper are in endless supply The variety of foods and drinks are endless. Classes of people include the Yonakas (Greeks), Kshatriyas, Indian warrior class; Brahmins and householders. The wives of the Greeks are delicate women. The Buddhist monks light up the city with their yellow robes like lamps, and bring down upon

the city, the breezes from the heights where the sages dwell.

In the spacious parks of Sakala, Yoga Masters and householders do a *Sun Salutation* and begin practising a set of over 900 yoga postures known. Standing poses; Inversions; Floor and Supine poses; Arm Balancing Poses; Twists and Seated poses; Breathing and Cleansing Practices and Resting poses. Some Yoga practitioners are seen standing on one leg. No one performs yoga postures or asanas without expert guidance and a doctor's medical clearance.

ALEXANDRIA, PTOLEMAIC EGYPT.

A Greek Merchant from Alexandria takes gold drachmas from his satchel and distributes it to the poor children of the city founded by Alexander the Great. His face is not shown. His bodyguards follow him. The merchant hands a large parcel to a courier destined for the Bactrian Greek King.

Alexandria was founded by Alexander the Great and constructed by his former bodyguard. Alexander encouraged respect for alien cultures and the open minded pursuit of knowledge. Tradition holds that he descended beneath the Red Sea in the world's first diving bell. He encouraged his generals and soldiers to marry Persian and Indian women. He respected the gods of other nations. He collected exotic lifeforms, including an elephant for Aristotle, his teacher. His city is constructed on a lavish scale, and designed to be the world centre for commerce, culture and learning. It is graced with broad avenues thirty meters wide, elegant architecture and statuary. Alexander's monumental tomb, and an enormous lighthouse, the Pharos, one of the seven wonders of the ancient world is seen.[1]

The Greek merchant descends into the world's largest library, the Alexandrian Library. Scholars consult over 500,000 scrolls studying various aspects of the entire universe, the *Cosmos*.[2] The Greek merchant passes the sections on physics, literature, medicine, astronomy, geography, philosophy, mathematics, biology and stops at engineering.

---

[1] Carl Sagan, *Cosmos: The Story of Cosmic Evolution, Science and Civilization*, London: Futura Books, 1991: 30-31.
[2] Carl Sagan, *Cosmos*, 1991: 30-31.

SAKALA CITY, KINGDOM OF BACTRIA.

A Royal Courier arrives with a parcel containing a scroll for the young general, Menander.

> Royal Courier:
> General Menander. A Greek Merchant from Alexandria sends you and your chief engineer a parcel anonymously.

Menander takes the scroll to a large table and unrolls it, placing weights on the corners of the introduction and contents. He reads it. He comes to drawings of spheres and their design.

> Menander:
> Euclid's *Optics and Catoptrics*.[3] It deals with the phenomena of reflected light and image forming optical systems using mirrors.

---

[3] Evangelos Spandagos ed. *Euclid, Optics and Catoptrics,* Athens, Aithra, 2000. In Greek.

175 BCE. HOUSE OF DIODOTUS AND HOUSE OF THE EUTHYDEMIDS. Menander the General enters the royal box, and sits next to his father, the aged Demetirus II, King of Bactria. Co-regent and soon to be new king Apollodotus I, and Demetrius I's sons, Agathocles and Pantaleon, who are sub-kings of Arachosia also enter. The bilingual mixed crowd of Bactrian Greeks and Indians roar as the Greek wrestler Davakos and the Indian wrestler Bala enter the arena. King Demetrius, looking tired, turns to his best general, Menander.

> Demetrius II, King of Bactria:
> Alexander's 20 city foundations have bloomed into 1,000 Bactrian-Greek cities. Consolidating the dominance of its Greek population. This is the reason why the Greco-Bactrian military class is strong enough to invade India.

> Menander the General:
> My King Demetrius, Alexander founded Greek colonies, whose citizens brought with them and continued to use the Greek language and religion, law and social customs. His gymnasia and national gymnasium training is the best means of preserving our special character.

> Demetrius II, King of Bactria:
> Remember, to preserve a Greek government,

based on the ruling family, the Greek military caste, and the Greek cities founded by Alexander. The key lies in treating all peoples with equality and justice. Greek justice in the towns and Hindu code in the rural areas. The Indians hate us. They also hate each other. The House of the Euthydemids is my legacy. The House of Eucratides must yield to our demands. The House of the Magadha is our greatest enemy.

Sub-King Agathocles:
General Menander, there's beauty and wisdom in both Greeks and Indians. The puzzle is trying to find it.

Sub-King Pantaleon:
My brother Agathocles, and I have initiated a program of bilingual coins which feature native Indian legends and celebrating the religion of Dionysus.

Sub-King Agathocles:
Pantaleon, the Indians love us, when an effort is made to communicate with them in their native tongue.

Sub-King Panteleon:
All our bilingual coins have both Greek script, Kharoshthi the script of Gandhara and Brahmi, the script of the Jumna and Ganges Valleys. Monetary

30

bilingualism and shared trade unites Greeks and Indians.

A WRESTLING MATCH.

Davakos and Bala grapple with each other and the mixed Indian and Greek crowd go wild.

> Narrator:
> Davakos and Bala are champion wrestlers having trained fanatically, in heat, snow, wind, rain, and storms. They have mastered forms such as the boar.

Davakos executes techniques involving courage, rushing, elbowing, kneeing and butting.

> Narrator:
> The Bull.

Bala executes techniques involving charging, tackling, and power striking.

> Narrator:
> The Cobra.

Davakos executes techniques involving attacking upper vital points.

> Narrator:
> The Deer.

Bala executes techniques involving alertness.

> Narrator:
>
> The Eagle.

Davakos executes techniques involving double hand blocking and striking.

> Narrator:
>
> The Monkey.

Bala executes techniques involving agility and confidence.

> Narrator:
>
> A paddy- bird.

Davakos executes techniques involving rapid flight.

> Narrator:
>
> The Panther.

Bala executes techniques involving circling, leaping, and tearing.

> Narrator:
>
> The Python.

Davakos executes techniques involving crushing, strangling, and gripping.

Narrator:

The Scorpion.

Bala executes techniques involving pinching and seizing nerve centres.

Narrator:

The Tiger.

Davakos executes techniques involving clawing and ripping.

Narrator:

And the viper.

Bala executes techniques involving attacking lower vital points. Bala defeated Davakos five years before and has trained at high-altitude under the best masters of all forms described. Davakos feints a right hook and Bala lunges forward. Davakos sweeps his left foot and Bala falls on his back. Davakos lands with an elbow to the chest and spins around, grabbing Bala in a choke hold. The crowd goes wild as Bala passes out. Davakos kisses his sleeping Indian giant and the referee raises his hand as victor.

MENANDER AND THE VENERABLE NAGASENA'S FIRST DISCUSSION.

General Menader goes to his window and watches the setting sun. No land on earth has

setting suns like India in summer. Menander's servant enters to announce the arrival of the

Buddhist Elder the Venerable Nagasena.

> Bactrian Servant:
> The Venerable Nagasena has arrived.

Venerable Nagasena enters.

> General Menander:
> Welcome Venerable Nagasena. I must prepare
> for battle, but I would like you to enjoy a meal with
> me. And later, we can discuss Buddhism.

> The Venerable Nagasena:
> And the schools of Greek philosophy.

Agathocleia, the daughter of the King Demetrius I, enters the royal box. She bows to the King and the co-regent King Apollodotus I and looks at General Menander with a look of love and longing and then remembers the royal protocol she must adhere to. King Demetrius and co-regent King Apollodotus I and sub-kings Agathocles and Pantaleon, smile and approve of her choice of husband.

Narrator:

Agathocleia, the daughter of King Demetrius I has chosen, General Menander to become her husband. The two had played King and Queen as children.

General Menander is served a cup of wine and glances in the direction of Agathocleia. He finds Agathocleia staring at him with her large and beautiful eyes. She lowers her gaze, as she recalls her royal protocol.

General Menander and the Venerable Nagasena enjoy a vegetarian meal and prepare for an intellectual discussion of East and Western philosophy. Menander wipes his mouth clean, followed by the Venerable Nagasena.

General Menander:
What is the Buddha's wisdom?

Venerable Nagasena:
Buddha's wisdom is broad as the ocean and His Spirit is full of great Compassion.

General Menander:
What form does the Buddha possess?

Agathocleia has snuck into Menander's Court and listens behind a large bronze mirror.

The Venerable Nagasena looks towards the bronze mirror momentarily, and turns to Menander once more.

> Venerable Nagasena:
> Buddha has no form but manifests Himself in Exquisiteness and leads us with His whole heart of Compassion.

> General Menander:
> Do you have any questions, Venerable Nagasena?

> Venerable Nagasena:
> Your birth and parentage.

> General Menander:
> I was born at the village of Kalasi, which lies not far from Alasanda (Alexandria of the Caucasus), about 200 yojanas (500 miles) from the city of Sakala. My father is Demetrius II, of the House of Diodotus.

The Venerable Nagasena and General Menander hear a noise behind the large screen, but continue their discussion.

> Venerable Nagasena:
> Many political leaders *talk* as philosopher kings before society.

Few *live* as philosopher kings who actually benefit society.

General Menander gets up, followed by the Venerable Nagasena, who hands him a large scroll. Agathocleia steps on a wooden step and views the Venerable Nagasena and Menander unrolling the large scroll and placing weights on the four corners of the vast map. Buddhist monasteries, cities, rivers, mountains, lakes and the names of major and minor ethnic groups are shown on the map. Agathocleia cannot hear what Nagasena and Menander are saying as they are whispering to each other.

A MAP OF BUDDHIST MONASTERIES IN INDIA.

Menander and his four closest advisers examine the map. The map shows the locations of all Buddhist monasteries throughout the Bactrian Empire and the Mauryan Empire in India.

>Devamantiya:
>The map shows all the Buddhist monasteries we must repair. The map can also be used as a network.

>Anantakaya:
>Major trading centres are included. Atranjikhera, Sringverpur, Jhunsi, Lakshagir, Ayodhya, and Sohagavra.

>Makura:
>Varanasi, and Buxar Chirand.

>Sabbadina:
>And the greatest trading centre of all –
>the capital of the Mauryan Empire,
>Pataliputra.

General Menander steps forward and points to another scroll he unravels which covers a large space over the map of Buddhist monasteries they were examining. It shows detailed military intelligence gathering on the Mauryan capital.

> General Menander:
> Pataliputra, the greatest city of India. In the district of the Prasians at the confluence of the Son and Ganges Rivers. Length of the city: 80 stades (9 miles). Breadth: 30 stades 1.4 miles). A long ditch is dug around the city 6 plethra in breath, thirty cubits deep. The wall has 570 towers and 64 gates. The thick walls are made of mud and timber.

Menander hears a noise behind the bronze mirror. He turns to his closest advisers.

> General Menander:
> Dismissed.

The four advisors exit the court. Menander walks up to the bronze mirror and pulls out Agathocleia. He embraces her.

> General Menander:
> Princess Agathocleia, I arrest you for spying on the king's general.

Princess Agathocleia:

General Menander, I'm just a Greek woman.

I'm not dangerous to the King's general.

Agathocleia kisses Menander passionately. They are in love, but keep their courtship private, following royal protocol.

Princess Agathocleia:

Emperor, Puryiamitra the usurper,

is your most dangerous opponent.

The Emperor supports the caste system

and the corrupt Brahmin religious order.

Menander nods affirmatively.

Princess Agathocleia:

Geneal Menander is the only man the Emperor of India fears. Menander must support and liberate the Buddhist Order from tyranny.

General Menander:

Your father controls 1,000 Bactrian Greek cities.

Each city has a Greek constitution, a council, a popular assembly and city magistrates.

Princess Agathocleia:

And you my general Menander, are its *soter,*
protector.

Menander and Agathocleia watch a magnificent Indian sun setting over the hills and mountains of Sakala in north-central India.

General Menander:
I want to promote the culture of both Greece
and India to the people.

Princess Agathocleia:
You will my love.

The Royal Courier arrives at the palace in Sakala, Bactria. The courier brings a parcel for general Menander.

The Royal Courier:
General Menander, a Greek merchant from
Alexandria, Egypt, sends you a gift.

The Royal Courier hands him the parcel and exits. Menander and Agathocleia open the parcel and finds a heavy scroll, containing the title of a celebrated scientific text. Menander reads it.

Menander:
Diocles' *On Burning Mirrors.*

Agathocleia:

A parabolic mirror focuses parallel light rays to a single point concentrating their power.

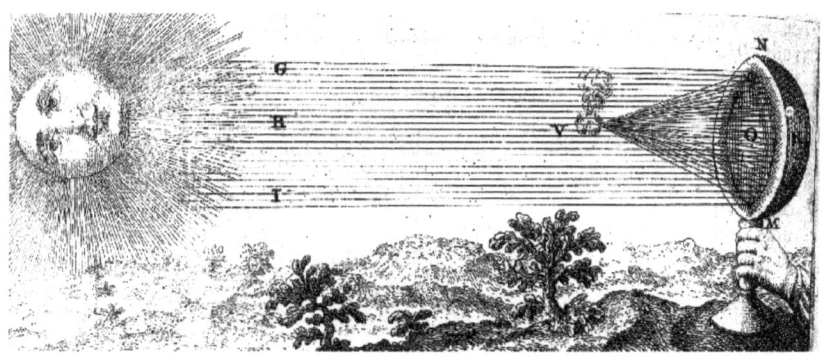

(Source: G. J. Toomer ed., *Diocles: On Burning Mirrors: The Arabic Translation of the Lost Greek Original,* Berlin: Heidelberg: Springer-Verlag, 1976.

Menander:

A wealthy Greek Merchant from Alexandria, Egypt keeps sending me scientific texts to strengthen Bactria.

Agathocleia:

Who is he?

Menander:

They say he is one of the most powerful Greek Merchants in the known world. Who he is, is still a mystery.

170-169 BCE. MENANDER ASCENDS THE THRONE AND BECOMES KING OF THE BACTRIAN EMPIRE. MENANDER'S WISDOM AND JUSTICE.

King Menander enters his court followed by his closest advisers, Devamantiya, Anantakaya, Makura and Sabbadina. Court officers bring in two women and two twin girls aged two.

>Devamantiya:
>Sire. The following case involves a dispute over who is the mother of the twin girls before the court.

Devamantiya brings the women before a statue of Pallas Athena holding the scales of justice.

>Devamantiya:
>Repeat after me. I, Cassiopeia of Nautika city do solemnly swear to tell the truth, the whole truth, and nothing but the truth, so help me Zeus.

>Cassiopeia of Nautika city:
>I, Cassiopeia of Nautika city, do solemnly swear to tell the truth, the whole truth and nothing but the truth so help me Zeus.

> Clytemnestra of Nautika city:
>
> I, Clytemnestra of Nautika city, do solemnly swear to tell the truth, the whole truth, and nothing but the truth so help me Zeus.

Menander scrutinizes both women. The eyes of a person a like a window into their soul.

> King Menander:
>
> Cassiopeia are you the lawful mother of the twin girls?

> Cassiopeia:
>
> Yes. Sire.

> King Menander:
>
> Clytemnestra are you the lawful mother of the twin girls?

> Clytemnestra:
>
> Yes. Sire.

> King Menander:
>
> Who is the mother of the twins?

King Menander and his four advisers look at each other and then, back at the women. Menander examines both women again. looks honest. Cassiopeia honest.

    King Menander:
    Cassiopeia, what is your husband's profession?

    Cassiopeia:
He works in the Silver mines.

    King Menander:
Clytemnestra, what is your husband's profession?

    Clytemnestra:
He works in the Copper mines.
    King Menander:
Cassiopeia, I ask you, one last time.
Are you the mother of the twin girls?

    Cassiopeia:
Yes. Sire.

    King Menander:
Clytemnestra, I ask you, one last time.
Are you the mother of the twin girls?

Clytemnestra:

Yes. Sire.

Menander suddenly rises from his throne. Pointing to the tall guard with the sword.

King Menander:

Execute the twins!!!!!

The false mother, Clytemnestra, does not protest or move. The real mother, Cassiopeia falls forward, onto her chest and stretches her hands, begging the King of Justice to suspend the death decree.

Cassiopeia:

Sire. Please don't kill my twins. Put me to death instead.

King Menander:

Cassiopeia, you are the lawful mother of the twins.

The twin girls run to their mother who lies prostrate before the King and hug her.

EMPEROR PUSHYAMITRA I INVADES THE INDO-GREEK KINGDOM IN THE BATTLE OF JALANDHAR CITY, NORTH-WEST INDIA.

King Menander:
Agathocleia, My Queen, I must prepare for battle.

Queen Agathocleia:
Defend Bactrria and destroy the Emperor.

Menander issues orders to his four closest advisers.

King Menander:
Mobilize the army to defend Jalandhar city. Concentric circles of my elite corp. of elephant drivers to defend the city in the formation I have prepared. All commanders of my divisions of chariot drivers to mobilize the horses and prepare them for battle. Infantry commanders to take positions and fortify each city gate.

Excurgus the Council Leader:
Iron tipped arrows at full capacity.

King Menander:
Excurgus. One million?

Excurgus the Council Leader:
One million.

169 BCE. EMPEROR PUSHYAMITRA I INVADES THE INDO-GREEK KINGDOM OF BACTRIA. THE BATTLE OF JALANDHAR CITY.

Emperor Pushyamitra invades the Indo-Greek city of Jalandhar with a force of 80,000 infantry and 1,000 elephants.

> Emperor Pushyamitra I:
> I, Emperor Pushyamtra I challenge general Menander the Bactrian Greek for the title of Maharajah of Maharajah's and Dharmarajah, King of Justice of India.

Emperor Pushyamitra I signals for his elite infantry commanders to start the cymbals and drums of war. The large Indian force invades Jalandhar City with wave after wave of archers aiming a sea of arrows into the city. Followed by chariot drivers attacking the main lines of the Indo-Greek army. Followed by elephant engagements which cause considerable damage to both sides. Menander signals for the Indo-Greek army to attack the left wing of the Emperor as it is perceptibly not in formation.

> King Menander:
> Charge!!!!

The Indo-Greek army advance as one body of elephants, chariot drivers, infantry and archers and mow down the invading army of the Emperor, systematically. Menander signals for his four closest advisers to catch the Emperor in a pincer movement. Menander's four advisers close in on the Emperor's forces and systematically mow down the Indian troops. The Emperor realizes that he has lost and turns his chariot and remaining forces back to his capital, Pataliputra, 1,000 miles away in the south of India. Menander watches him leave.

>King Menander:
>The Emperor will be back. Excurgus, start production of eight types of iron tipped arrows I've requested.

The Emperor's son, Crown Prince Agnimitra and his young son Vasumitra lead a unit of Mauryan infantry up the hill and smash through a line of Bactrian Greeks who are both surprised and astonished. Menander spots them and goes after them. Crown Prince Agnimitra and his son Vasumitra show exceptional swordsmanship against the Greeks before escaping before Menander's large and celebrated Bactrian cavalry who finish off all remaining Mauryan infantry.

Menander's four closest advisers enter the King's headquarters following the victory and repulsion of Emperor Pushyamitra I's forces from Jalandhar city.

>King Menander:
>Devamantiya, you're in charge of the production of type 1 and type 2 iron tipped arrows.

Devamantiya:
Type 1 arrow head, leaf shaped blade, and rhombic cross section, with prominent mid-rib running from shank to blade point, double tanged. Type 2 arrow head, leaf shaped blade, with square cross section, with a long shank, double-tanged. 200,000 each.

King Menander:
Anantakaya, you're in charge of the production of type 3 and 4 iron tipped arrows.

Anantakaya:
Type 3 arrow head, leaf shaped blade, triangular cross section, and double tanged. Type 4 arrow head narrowing leaf shaped blade, lozenge cross section, long shank, double-tanged. 200,000 each.

King Menander:
Makura, you're in charge of type 5 and 6.

Makura:
Type 5 arrow head, knife blade, lozenge cross section, double-tanged. Type 6 arrow head, triangular leaf-shaped

blade, lozenge cross-section, long-shank, double-tanged. 200,000 each.

King Menander:
Sabbadina, you're in charge of type 7 and 8.

Sabbadina:
Type 7 arrow head forked point head, rhombic cross section, long shank, double tanged. Type 8 arrow head, leaf-shaped blade, rhombic cross –section, short thickened shank, double tanged. 200,000 each.

King Menander:
Chief Engineer, you're in charge of the production of my siege engines.

Menander hands him a list of siege engines to be constructed on a scroll. The Chief Engineer's eyes grow wide with horror and anticipation and finally with understanding at the enterprise the King has in store for Emperor Pushyamitra, the destroyer of Buddhist monasteries and violator of the *Dharma*, the law of equality.

170 – 165 BC. THE HOUSE OF EUCRATIDES, WESTERN BACTRIA, INDIA.

>Narrator:
>Eucratides began his reign in Western Bactria in 168 BC. He fought several battles with Demetrius II and suffered heavy losses, but always found a way to escape. A soldier of fortune, he built up his wealth by great victories in Sogdiana, Aria, Arachosia and India. His goal, to control the main trade route out of India, the Kabul valley. Eucratides's next target is the great trading city of Taxila. Menander is ready to defend Taxila.

Menander rides out with his four advisers and some Bactrian Greek troops to observe the movements of the rebel Eucratides and his army.

>Menander:
>Are my men in possession of the passes in the mountains?

>Devamantiya:
>Yes general.

>Menander:

Are all my men in possession of the 24 largest towns of Bactria?

Anantakaya:
Yes, general.

Menander:
Have the Astacenians and Assacenians between the Rivers Indus and Cophen committed to our defence?

Makura:
Yes, general.

Trumpets sound as Eucratides approaches Taxila city.

Eucratides:
No prisoners!

Eucratides attacks with the bulk of his cavalry. Menander has divided his Bactrian Greek troops into four units of 20,000 strong. Menander's trumpeters sound for his army of elephants to route Eucratides's army from the valley below and the high ground to the north. The two armies clash. Chariot drivers from both armies' clash. Menander's elephant craft is superior. Eucratides tries to encircle Taxila city. Menander counters with a combination of archers and fine horsemanship from his Persian crack infantry. Eucratides goes for the main gate. Menander attacks Eucratides from the right front. A desperate battle of attrition takes place. Missiles from both sides are fired into both camps. Burning chariots are driven into the gates of Taxila city. Menander's trumpeters sound a second attack with his cavalry closing in on Eucratides's main force from both sides. Menander deals a Eucratides a crushing blow. Eucratides, with the bulk of his army destroyed, makes good his escape into the hills. Menander's army chases him into the mountains but Eucratides, is no-where to be found.

> Menander:
> Eucratides knows the Bactrian lands better than anyone. One day, I will get you old fox.

> Narrator:
> Menander consolidates his power in Bactria and fortifies over 200 Bactrian cities. Menander also assumes the leadership of the united clans of the Houses of Diodotus, and Euthydemus. Stratagems, tactics and chess are Menander's forte.

THE HOUSE OF MAGADHA, THE MAURYAN EMPEROR PUSHYAMITRA.

An eagle flies down the Ganges River, the greatest river in India towards the capital Pataliputra. It circles the 570 towers and 64 gates of the great city and flies towards the palace of the Mauryan Emperor, Pushyamitra I. Ostriches with their colourful feathers surround the courtyards. Indian bazaars abound selling almost everything under the sun. Inside the palace, a magnificent display of wealth and power is showcased by the Royal Magadhan Court. Diamonds, rubies, gems and sapphires adorn the dress and attire of the Royal Mauryan Family. Pushyamitra's Chief Adviser approaches the Emperor.

> Crown Prince Agnimitra:
> Father, I have something to show you.

The Emperor Pushyamitra and his son go towards the eastern window of the palace and gaze into the bazaar down below. The Crown Prince points into the crowd at the entrance, disguised as traders.

> Crown Prince Agnimitra:
> Look there. General Menander and his four closest advisers are in the market place, disguised as traders from the north.

> Emperor Pushyamitra:
> Menander the Bactrian- Greek? Son, you are Crown Prince Agnimitra. Follow him.

Crown Prince Agnimitra:
My agents are on to him.

Menander and his four closest advisers notice the two figures on the eastern terrace staring at them. Menander and his advisers go down an alley way and enter a store owned by one of his governors. The Emperor's agents also enter the store but find no trace of Menander or his advisers.

The Emperor's Agents question the governor's shop keeper.

The Emperor's Agent:
We're did the Bactrian Greek go?

The Shop Keeper:
I gave him the price of this gold chain
and he rejected my offer. He went out
that door.

The Emperor's Agent's look around. They exist through the door and look up and down the street and along the bazaar. Menander and his advisers have disappeared. The agents look up at the Emperor's eastern terrace and nod negatively.

Emperor Pushyamitra I:
Summon my advisers.

The Emperor's Chief Adviser bows low and exists. Moments later, 100 Senior Military Advisers convene in Emperor Pushyamitra's Court.

> Emperor Pushyamitra I:
> Menander the Bactrian Greek general was seen in Pataliputra, with his advisers, disguised as traders.
>
> Pushyamitra's Chief Military Adviser:
> Menander has a dream. Alexander's dream of conquering the greatest Indian city, Pataliputra.
>
> Emperor Pushyamitra I:
> Alexander defeated the great Porus, Rajah of the Punjab. His troops refused to advance beyond the Beas River. Agrammes who ruled Pataliputra at the time, stood waiting, for Alexander with 80,000 cavalry, 200,000 infantry and 1,000 elephants. No Greek has ever won the capital. I have 200,000 troops, with another 200,000 on call. Menander defended Jalandhar city. But I shall destroy him, next time.
>
> Pushyamitra's Chief Military Adviser:
> The Bactrian Greeks claim India because 2,000 years ago, Dionysus conquered India. Sanskrit, the language of the gods was formed by the Indo-Europeans who encountered the native Indians of the south, around 1750 BCE. A

fruitful encounter.

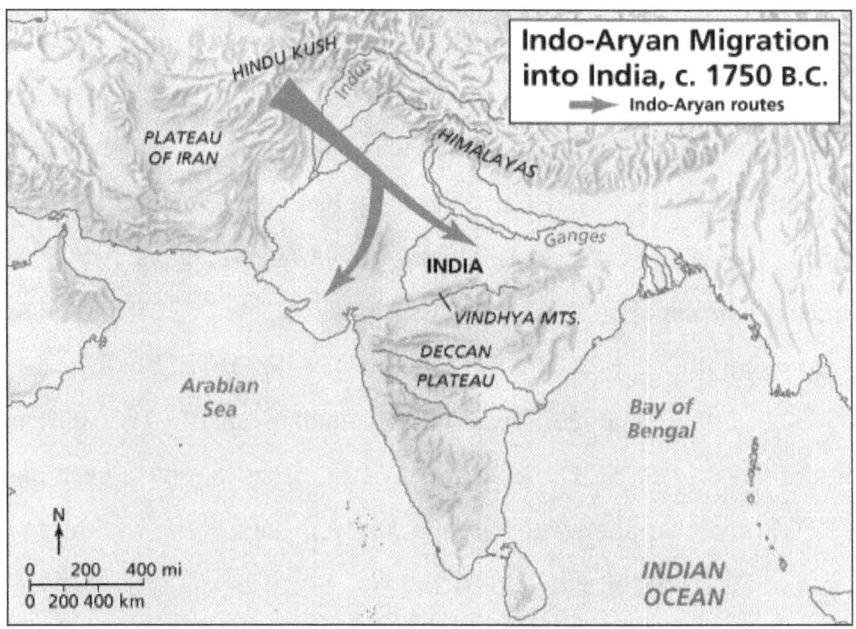

(Source: *Bactrian Origin. Indo-European Invasion, 1750 BCE*. URL: www.googlemaps.com/Menander's Empire, Accessed 10/04/2018).

Emperor Pushyamitra walks towards a tall wall, depicting the faces of 157 Indian Kings, who ruled India for the last 3,000 years. Some Emperors who can be seen on the wall are: The Pradyota Dynasty Kings who reigned for 138 years from 799-684 BCE. They are: Pradyota Mahasena; Palaka; Visakhayupa; Ajaka; and Varttivarddhana. The Haryanka Dynasty Kings who reigned from 566 to 413 BCE. They are: Bimbisara 544-492 BCE; Ajatashatru 492-460 BCE; Udayin 460-440 BCE; Anuruddha; Munda and Nagadasaka 437-413 BCE. The Shishunaga Dynasty Kings from 413-345 BCE. They are: Shishunaga 413-395 BCE; Kakavarna Kalashoka 395 who reigned with his sons for 42 years; Bhadrasena;

Korandavarna; Mangura; Sarvanjaha; Jalika; Ubhaka; Sanjaya; Koravya; Panchamaka; Nandivardhana and Mahanadin 367-345 BCE. The Nanda Dynasty Kings from 345-321 BCE; Ugrasena, Panduka, Pandugati, Bhutapala, Rashtrapala, Govishanaka, Dashasiddhaka, Kaivarta and Dhana also known as Agrammes. Chandragupta 321-298 BCE; Bindusara 298-272 BCE; Ashoka 268-232; Dasharatha 232-224 BCE; Samprati 224-215 BCE; Shalishuka 215-202 BCE; Devavaman 202-195 BCE; Shatadhanvan 195-187 BCE and Brihadratha 187-184 BCE. The opposite wall has faces that have been painted over with white pink colour. They are the *Yavanas* the Greeks who ruled India in the time of Dionysus circa 1,500 BCE.

Emperor Pushyamitra I:
I am the Emperor Pushyamitra I. 157 Indian Kings have ruled India over 3,000 years. Alexander's dream of conquering the Ganges Valley and our capital Pataliputra shall become Menander's nightmare. Let him come and test my strength and power. I will show Menander the Bactrian Greek, the *real* India.

The Emperor's 100 Military Advisers shout in unison, Indian slogans and wave their fists in the air in defiance of the Bactrian Greeks.

Menander and his four closest advisers disguised as traders enter the celebrated Buddhist Monastery of Kukkutarama in Pataliputra. The Venerable Elder welcomes them. Menander and his advisers insist on serving all the monks for their evening meal. Menander holds a large wooden spoon, and serves lentils to the monks from a bucket holding the stew from Devamantiya. Anantakaya serves naan bread. Makura serves fruit and Sabbadina serves vegetables.

A WEALTHY GREEK MERCHANT

The wealthy Greek Merchant who is secretly supporting general Menander, walks the palace grounds of the Mauryan Empire in Pataliputra. His face is not shown. He distributes gold drachmas to children as he enters a chariot and is driven around the architectural wonders of the capital. The Greek Merchant belongs to an elite group of men and women who control trading routes throughout the known world.

(Source: *Ancient Greek Gold Coin of King Alexander the Great, 323 BC,* URL: https://www.vcoins.com/Gold Coin of Alexander the Great/ Accessed 04042018).

EMPEROR PUSHYAMITRA I PERSECUTES BUDDHIST ORDERS AND SUPPORTS THE BRAHMIN FACTION FROM THE CAPITAL, PATALIPUTRA, GANGES VALLEY.

Suddenly, a wounded monk who has been attacked with clubs, arrows and severe burns to his body, enters the compound and collapses at the door of the monk's eating quarters. Menander and his four advisers look at the Buddhist monks' burns. The Venerable Elder goes to the aid of the fallen monk, along with other monks.

>Venerable Elder of the Monastery of Kukkutarama: Brother, who did this to you?

>Injured Buddhist Monk:
>The Brahmin Faction supported by the Emperor of Magadha, Pushyamitra.

Menander gets his medicine bag and administers some healing ointments on to the burns of the injured monk.

>General Menander:
>Rest brother. I will deal with the Brahmin faction.

>The Venerable Elder:
>We do not condone violence, brother.

>General Menander:
>To fight creatures of violence, you need, creatures

of violence. I give you my word, I shall be swift.

Menander gives his advisers a determined look. They know what they must do and make appropriate actions against the Emperor of Magadha's secret security force.

CROWN PRINCE AGNIMITRA'S APPETITES AND INTRIGUES.

> Narrator:
> The Emperor's son, Crown Prince Agnimitra is known for his bravery, intelligence and appetites for European women and precious stones.

Crown Prince Agnimitra is in his *pleasure palace* in Pataliputra. He comes to the balcony and admires the view of the greatest city in India, Pataliputra. Behind him, beautiful womeninvite him to bed.

> European Concubine:
> Prince Agnimitra, come, join us.

The Crown Prince looks at the beautiful women in his bed. Business like, he orders them to leave.

> Crown Prince Agnimitra:
> You must leave now. My father, the Emperor is on his way.

Emperor Pushyamitra arrives at the Crown Princes' Bedchamber and looks at the beautiful departing women with distaste at his son's appetites.

Emperor Pushyamitra I:
Son, you're appetite for European women and precious stones will be your undoing.

Crown Prince Agnimitra:
Father, your persecution of Buddhist Monks shall be your own doom. Why don't you take lessons from illustrious predecessors and seek friendship and trade with the Greeks?

Emperor Pushyamtra I:
Son, one victor can stand victorious, one Emperor, one King of Justice in India.

Crown Prince Agnimitra:
Take a lesson from the friendship of Alexander and Rajah Porus. The friendship between Chandragupta and Seleucus. The friendship between Antiochus and Sophagasenes. An alliance built on friendship and trade make India great.

Emperor Pushyamtra I a ruthless and driven man, looks his son in the eyes.

Emperor Pushyamitra I:
I started my career as the Rajah of Vidasa. Do you know how many enemies tried to take, what I won, through courage and sacrifice? Life is a contest. And this contest will end with the death of Menander or the Emperor. *I am* God's Minister on Earth.

MENANDER'S RECONNAISANCE MISSION IN CHIRAND CITY, EAST OF THE GANGES VALLEY.

Narrator:

General Menander and his four closest advisers, disguised as traders, continue their reconnaissance mission in Chirand, a large town with a population ranging from 50,000 and 100,000. The House of Euthydemids, King Demerius, his two sons, Agathocles and Pantaleon have established strong business networks in the area.

Menander and his advisers notice Emperor Pushyamitra's Secret Security Force following a discreet distance. Menander and his advisors go into a coffee shop. and order something to eat.

Menander:

The Emperor's Secret Security Force has spotted us. Time to change our appearance.

Menander and his advisers go into a safe house and dress up as women. They leave the safe house at 10 minute intervals, and meet at a hill station, north of Chirand. The Emperor's Secret Security Force has lost them in the crowd celebrating *Diwali the Festival of Lights*. Menander and his advisers change back into the clothes of merchants.

Devamantiya:

General, you look handsome tonight.

Anantakaya:

General, Chirand has 500 elephants and an infantry of 50,000. All loyal to the Emperor.

Makura:

General, Chirand has 27 bridges.

Sabbadina:

The people are loyal to the usurper.
The Emperor has paid huge sums in
gold to secure their loyalty. Most of
the people are loyal to the Brahminic
faction.

A crowd goes wild in panic as a Buddhist monastery in the hills is set on fire. Menander andhis advisers approach some locals to ask what has happened.

Menander:

Who started the fire, friend?

Local Merchant:

The Emperor's hand is behind it all.
He is supplying the Brahminic faction with
weapons and soldiers to set fire to Buddhist
compounds. I hope the tyrant is overthrown
one day. However, the Emperor is too powerful.

Local Merchant:
Only one man, can defeat that tyrant.
General Menander, the Bactrian Greek.

Menander's face grows in admiration, then seriousness as he and his advisers leave for the city of Buxar. The wealthy Greek Merchant who secretly supports Menander follows him to Chirand city. He distributes gold drachmas to the children of the bazaars. Then he disappears into a chariot and is driven away.

MENANDER'S RECONNAISANCE MISSION IN BUXAR CITY, THE GANGES VALLEY.

Menander and his advisers enter an arena to watch two local champions in wrestling, compete and conduct their reconnaissance mission in Buxar city. It is May and the temperature hovers at 35 degrees Celsius or 95 Fahrenheit. The wealthy Greek Merchant is in the crowd also.

> Menander:
> I put 1 Gold talent on the Greek wrestler.

> Devamantiya:
> I put 2 Gold talents on the Indian wrestler.
> General, look east.

Menander spots the Emperor of Magadha's Secret Security Forces scrutinizing the faces of the crowd. One by one, Menander's party leave just as the wrestling match commences. They enter a narrow street lane and are confronted by the Emperor of Magadha's Secret Security Forces.

> The Emperor's Secret Security Officer:
> Welcome to Buxar city General Menander.

The Emperor of Magadha's Secret Security Forces draw daggers and attack Menander and his advisers. Menander grabs the largest of the five attackers and strikes his throat, breaking his assailants' thorax. Makura punches his attacker repeatedly and runs the man through with his sword. Devamantiya head butts his attacker repeatedly and then runs his sword through the man. Sabbadina is enjoying a bag of Indian sweets and just watches the small victory.

>Sabbadina:
>General, Buxar also has 500 elephants and an infantry of 50,000. All loyal to the Emperor.

MENANDER'S RECONNAISANCE MISSION IN AYODHYA CITY, THE GANGES VALLEY.

Menander and his four advisers drive a chariot into the Ayodhya city, famous for its Hindu temples and architecture. A chorus of Hindu devotees sing the *Gayatri mantra*[4], an invocation to the sun as a symbol of rebirth and renewal in the shade of the great temple. In June, the temperature hovers at 40 degrees Celsius or 104 Fahrenheit and 50 degrees Celsius or 122 Fahrenheit. A Buddhist Elder approaches Menander and his men.

> Venerable Elder of Ayodhya Buddhist Order:
> My good man. Follow me.

Menander and his advisers scrutinize the Venerable Elder for a moment.

> Venerable Elder of Ayodhya Buddhist Order:
> The Venerable Nagasena is waiting for you.

Menander and his advisers smile and enter the Buddhist compound. They are all greeted by the Venerable Nagasena who proceeds to feed all of Menander's party personally.

> Menander:
> Venerable Nagasena, what brings you to
> Ayodhya, the city of temples?

---

[4] Judith Sankaranarayan, *Many Voices, One Song*, (New Dehlhi: Radha Soami Satsang Beas, 2013): 337.

Venerable Nagasena:
We have not concluded our discussion about
the nature of existence.

Menander:
Ashoka, the greatest Mauryan Emperor
believed that the welfare and happiness of
of his subjects to be of the highest importance.

Venerable Nagasena:
Ashoka was also half Greek. And the greatest
benefactor of Buddhism in India. To become
Maharaja of Maharajas and Dharmaraja the King
of Justice is the greatest of achievements, provided
it reflects the will of a moral and noble population.

Menander notices his four closest advisers getting up to leave and bowing to the Venerable Nagasena.

Menander:
Venerable Nagasena, I must retire.
Can I meet you in Delhi to continue our
discussion of the nature of existence.

The Venerable Nagasena and Menander rise and both bow to each other and depart.

Anatakaya:

Ayodhya has 2000 elephants.

Devamantiya:

10,000 horses.

Makura:

20,000 chariots.

Sabbadina:

With an Indian infantry of 100,000, and only half are loyal to the Emperor. The Royal Courier has arrived.

The Royal Courier bows before Menander and hands him a parcel. Menander opens it and finds another large and heavy scroll. He reads the title of the text.

Menander:

Another scroll. The Greek Merchant from Alexandria is still a mystery to me.

He opens the scroll further. He opens another empty scroll to make drawings and notes as he reads the text.

Menander:

Archimedes' *On Burning Mirrors*. A parabola has a focus, parallel rays of light are concentrated at one point. The mirror required has the form of the surface known as a paraboloid of revolution. A sufficiently good approximation to that surface can be obtained by a set of plane mirror; although, once the approximate form has been obtained, empirical adjustments will find most efficient shape. The actual design depends on knowing that the radiant flux at the focus produced by a given mirror decreases with increasing focal length and that there is a limiting distance beyond which ignition will not take place. And in construction depends on having some means of setting up and operating such a mirror.

Menander looks at his four closest advisers.

Menander:

The Chief Engineer must design a *paraboloidal burning mirror*. Concave mirrors of bronze covered with silver and lead.[5] The only worthy targets are the wooden and mud city walls. About 20 cities have such walls. We must get within 50 metres of the city walls.

---

[5] Simms, D. L. "Archimedes and the Burning Mirrors of Syracuse." *Technology and Culture* 18, no. 1 (1977): 1-24. doi:10.2307/3103202.

Devamantiya:

The Chief Engineer has knowledge of conic sections.

Anantakaya:

There are three types of cones: obtuse, right-angled and acute.

Makura:

The parabola, ellipse and hyperbola.

Sabbadina:

Parabolas pass through conic sections which intersect each other.

Menander:

Multiply the mirror surface diameter by 7 or 49 and it will increase the effective focal length of the sun's rays. And find out who on earth the Greek Merchant from Alexandria is who is helping us, or himself.

Menander:

Sections of a parabola; sections of a hyperbola and sections of an ellipse.

The Chief Engineer arrives and greets the King.

Chief Engineer:

Sire.

Menander:

Can you design a paraboloidal burning mirror?

Chief Engineer:

Sire. I can bring down the sun. To construct a burning mirror of a given focal length is done by drawing a parabola by means of focus and directrix.

Menander:

Elaborate.

Chief Engineer:

Let us say that we want to construct 570 burning mirrors to destroy the 570 towers of the walls of the capital, Pataliputra. I would focus on generating as many curves as possible. Each burning mirror will be made of sections of parabola; sections of hyperbola and sections of an ellipse.

> Menander:
> What has the Royal Courier brought you?

The Chief Engineer opens the large scroll and shows the King and his Advisers specific drawings relating to the construction of a burning mirror.

> Chief Engineer:
> A Greek Merchant from Alexandria has sent me a scroll by Diocles' *On Burning Mirrors*. Diocles' explains that the three sections are obtained by cutting a right circular cone by a plane at right angles to a generator. If the cone is right angled this produces a parabola. If obtuse angled a hyperbola. If acute angled an ellipse. I shall employ Algebraic Geometry and the cissoids formula $y^2 = x^3/(2a - x)$.[6]

> Menander:
> In addition to the 570 burning mirrors for the towers, I also want 64 burning mirrors of larger surface and multiplied with a magnitude and focus to harness the sun's rays and increase it to the point of burning the main gates of the capital. Sire, I shall construct the order required and get back to you.

The Chief Engineer nods and leaves. The wealthy Greek Merchant from

---

[6] *Cissoid of Diocles*, http://www-history.mcs.st-andrews.ac.uk/Curves/Cissoid.html Accessed 03042018.

Alexandria, who is flanked by his bodyguards, walks through a narrow bazaar and distributes gold coins to the children of the city.

MENANDER'S RECONNAISANCE MISSION IN SOHGAURA CITY, EAST OF THE GANGES VALLEY.

General Menander and his closest advisers ride their horses into Sohgaura city, east of the Ganges Valley. It is October, the weather is warm and pleasant with a tinge of humidity. A row of small shop keepers' sell spices, clothes, jewellery and handcrafts. A leading musician known as a *Kirtana* gives a *kirtana* performance. Accompaniment of regionally popular musical instruments, such as the *harmonium*, the *veena*, a form of stringed instrument, the *tabla,* a one-sided drum, the *pakhawaj* or two-sided drum, flute and *talas* or cymbals combine with the melodious voice of the leading Kirtana to recite the *Gayatri mantra*, from the *Samhita Hymns*, the most ancient Vedic texts. In unison they sing:

> Kirtana and Musicians:
> We cry out for you, hero, like unmilked cows to
> the lord of the living world.
> To the Lord of the unmoving world whose eye is
> the sun, o Indra.!!![7]

Just then, Menander and his advisers, hungry after their long journey, enter an eatery and tip the lead Kirtana musician. Menander orders a Jaipur style Mung Dal. Devamantiya orders Rice with Green Peas and Almonds. Anantakaya orders North Indian Curried

---

[7] Frits Staal, *Discovering the Vedas: Origins, Mantras, Rituals, Insights*, (New Delhi, Penguin Books, 2009): 107- 115.

Cauliflower and Potatoes. Makura the Persian, orders Creamed Spinach with Curd Cheese known as Palak Panir. Sabbadina the Anatolian orders his favourite dish, Griddle Baked Bread or Chapati with yoghurt.

Menander:
Sohgaura has an infantry of 50,000 and a cavalry of 50,000. Half loyal to the Emperor. The others, undecided.

Devamantiya:
And 25,000 chariots and horses.

Anantakaya:
The number of storekeepers is 5,000.

Sabbadina:
And 500 elephants.

A Buddhist monk enters the eatery and approaches general Menander. The General and his four advisers look up.

A Buddhist Emissary:
General Menander, I am a Bhikkhu Bodhi.
I bring a message from the Venerable Nagasena.

The Buddhist monk gives the message to Menander who opens it and reads it. He looks up at his party.

> Menander:
> The Venerable Nagasena says that it is
> not safe for us to stay in Sohgaura city.
> He wants to meet us in Ahichhatra city
> and escort us to Mathura and then on to Delhi.

Menander's party rises and pays for their meal and exit the eatery. The Emperor's Secret Security Force follows the Buddhist monk who is escorting Menander and his men, down a narrow laneway in Sohgaura city. Menander spots them and alerts his men. Menander's party walk up a hill and reach a Buddhist monastery and hide from the security force. Once the Emperor's Security Force passes a narrow pathway, Menander jumps on to the first security officer and bangs his head against the Buddhist bronze gong. His advisers follow suit, banging their assailants' heads against the bronze gongs of the Buddhist monastery compound. Inside, Buddhist monks chant in unison: *Om Mani Padme Om* continuously.

> Bhikkhu Bodhi:
> The Emperor of Magadha is a ruthless tyrant.
> He has a vast security force searching for you.
> Please take this boat up the Ghaghara River to
> Ahichhatra city. The Venerable Nagasena is waiting
> for you there.

Menander and his party bow to Bhikku Bodhi and depart on the boat up river. The wealthy Greek merchant and his entourage walk through a bazaar. The merchant distributes gold drachmas to the children. He observes Menander in action and nods his head affirmatively. Menander is the one who can restore India to Ashoka's ethical and moral standard and wipe out the economic parasites along the Ganges and Jumna rivers who are bleeding India dry.

EMPEROR PUSHYAMITRA'S INTELLIGENCE NETWORK REPORT.

Crown Prince Agnimitra enters the palace of the Emperor of Magadha and stands before the usurper, Pushyamitra I.

>Emperor Pushyamitra I:
>Son, what do you report?

>Crown Prince Agnimitra:
>General Menander is personally leading a reconnaissance of the central and eastern parts of the Magadha Empire. His closest advisers have been identified as Devamantiya, whose real name is Demetrius, a Greek. Anantakaya, whose real name is Antiochus, is also a Greek. Makura is an Iranian. And Sabbadina is an Anatolian. All of them are career military men.

>Emperor Pushyamitra I:
>Have our efforts to infiltrate Menander's Council of 500 been successful?

>Crown Prince Agnimitra:
>No.

Emperor Pushyamitra I:
Have our efforts to infiltrate the Greek Military Elite been successful?

Crown Prince Agnimitra:
No.

Emperor Pushyamitra I:
Continue to clandestinely support the Brahmin faction and persecute the Buddhist Orders throughout my Empire. I want the Brahmin faction and the caste system to prevail.

Crown Prince Agnimitra:
Yes, father.

Emperor Pushyamitra I:
Bring the Greek spy to me.

Menander's Greek spy is brought it before the Emperor Pushyamitra I.

Emperor Pushyamitra I:
You are General Menander's spy. Your mission has failed.

Menander's Spy:
You are General Pushyamitra, the usurper who assassinated the legitimate Mauryan Emperor Brihadratha. You have violated the law of Dharma. Death to tyrants!!!!

Emperor Pushyamitra I:
You are also a Buddhist. I am the Maharaja of Maharajas the King of Kings. I am the Dharmaraja the King of Justice. The law of Dharma and the law of Karma does not apply to the Emperor.

Emperor Pushyamitra I nod's affirmatively for Menander's spy to be executed. The Greek spy's ankles and hands are chained and tied to four elephants who are marched outwards until the Greek spy is torn from limb to limb. The execution is witnessed by all the people and show them that to oppose the Emperor Pushyamitra I is to invite certain death. Buddhist Monasteries are set on fire. Crops, burnt. Monks, beaten with wooden clubs and thrown off cliffs.

MENANDER'S RECONNAISANCE MISSION IN AHICHHATRA CITY, NORTH OF THE GANGES VALLEY.

Menander and his four advisers enter Ahichhatra city, population 100,000. The main road is full of store keepers selling almost everything under the sun. Musicians comprising a folk band made up of instruments such as the drum, cymbal, flute and lute and a female mezzo-soprano sings beautiful *abhangs* or short devotional songs in praise of the Hindu god Vithoba, in the Marathi language.[8] A Buddhist monk approaches Menander and his party.

> Buddhist Monk of Ahichhatra:
> Welcome General Menander. Please follow me.

Menander and his party follow the monk down the main road. Then turns down a narrow alleyway. Overhead is a hill with a series of terraces. The Emperor's Secret Security Force has paid a lot of gold for Brahmin factions to identify and eliminate general Menander and his party. A Brahmin priest who is corrupt, spots the Bactrian Greek and his party. He has travelled to Sakala in the north and seen the general from a close distance. The Brahmin priest notifies the Emperor's Secret Security Forces and they set on fire some long baskets full of hay and roll them down- hill. The long baskets on fire roll towards Menander's party. At the last minute, the Buddhist monk, spots the baskets rolling down hill on fire and in line to fall on to the general's party. He pushes the general out of the way and shouts at his party

---

[8] Judith Sankaranarayan, *Many Voices, One Song*, (New Delhi, Radha Soami Satsang Beas, 2013): 72-75.

to dive out of the way, which they do, just in time. The baskets on fire land and set on fire a store keeper's apartment. The Buddhist monk helps Menander to his feet and the entire party disappears down a maze of alley ways to a Buddhist monastery in the hills. The Venerable Nagasena is waiting for Menander and his party, inside the compound. The two bow to each other, followed by Menander's party.

>Venerable Nagasena:
>Welcome to Ahichhatra city, general Menander.

>Menander:
>Venerable Nagasena, it's my pleasure.

A group of Greek and Indian merchants enter and bow low to the Venerable Elder.

>Venerable Nagasena:
>Before you leave for Mathura city, speak with
>the merchants who have arrived.

>Menander:
>Venerable Nagasena, I have read some of
>the Buddhist texts. I would like to know how
>one controls the 108 modes of feeling?

Outside, the Emperor's Secret Security Force searches each store keeper's apartment for General Menander and his party. They go down as many narrow laneways in Ahichhatra city as possible, without result.

> Venerable Nagasena:
> And that is how you control 108 modes of feeling. My guides will take you and your party through the jungle. A boatman who belongs to our Order shall take you across the Ganges River to Mathura. I shall call on you in Krishna's city.

The Venerable Nagasena and Menander and his party rise and bow to the Elder and take leave with the guide assigned to them.

EMPEROR PUSHYAMITRA I TRAVELS DOWN THE RIVER SIND TO HIS ANCESTRAL HOME IN VIDISA, SOUTH-WEST OF THE CAPITAL PATALIPUTRA.

Pushyamitra I, his adult son, Crown Prince Agnimitra and his young son Vasumitra, sail on the royal Mauryan barge towards Vidisa city, the emperor's ancestral home. His Chief Military Adviser is with him.

>Emperor Pushyamitra I:
>Chief of Military Advisers, what report do you have on general Menander?

>Chief of Military Advisers:
>Menander and his four closest military advisers are still between Ahichhatra city and Mathura.

>Emperor Pushyamitra I:
>The Bactrian Greeks are no match for our forces. We outnumber then 4 to 1. Keep me informed of Menander's movements. Continue to support the Brahminic faction and secretly persecute the Buddhist Order. We have virtually wiped out Buddhism in north-eastern India.

The Chief of Military Advisers bows and takes his leave. The Emperor's Royal Bodyguards comprising Greek Women accompany him as he walks up and down the Royal Barge.

THE EMPEROR'S TROOPS, NORTHWEST OF THE GANGES VALLEY.

Dusk is approaching as Menander, his four advisers and their Buddhist guide travel through the jungle leading to Mathura city. Suddenly, the heavy sound of soldiers marching is heard. The Buddhist Monk runs up to Menander and his party.

> Buddhist Monk:
> General Menander, the Emperor's troops are marching through this forest. We must hide in the tiger's cave.

Menander and his party enter a narrow pathway leading down to a cave system. Above them, the sound of the Emperor's troops passing overhead is heard. The last of the Emperor's soldier hears a branch breaking. He stops and tries to listen for the origin of the sound. Menander and his party can see the soldier from a hole in the ground. The soldier decides that it is nothing and hurries back to marching with the main column of the Emperor's troops.

> Menander:
> Have they passed?

> Buddhist Monk:
> Yes general.

Behind them a tiger awakens from a long sleep, after feasting on the remains of an elephant.

It makes a slow but growing growl sound. The tiger approaches the Buddhist monk who is busy repeating a Buddhist mantra. Menander and his party don't make a sound. The tiger smells each one of the men. It licks Menander's face and departs through the entrance. Tigers are known for being more powerful than elephants. To survive a close encounter with one, is nothing short of remarkable.

MATHURA CITY, KRISHNA'S BIRTHPLACE. THE CITY OF TEMPLES.

Menander, accompanied by his four advisers and the Buddhist monk, acting as their guide reach the mighty Ganges, the greatest river in all of India. They board, a boat and the Buddhist monk, paddles towards Atranjikhera city. An old Buddhist insists on boarding a boat and is welcomed by all. The old Buddhist begins to speak in ancient Sanskrit, using very ancient Greek, not spoken in over 2500 years. *Kirtans* or singing of hymns to the accompaniment of music is performed on the main road in the city.

Menander:
The old Buddhist is using Greek I have never heard before. What is he saying?

Buddhist Monk and Guide:
He is telling the story of the time of the Kuru Dynasty and the great battle between the House of Dhrtarastra and the House of the Pandavas which happened almost 2500 years ago. Terrible weapons wiped out both sides.

Menander:
He's using very old Greek. What's he saying?

Buddhist Monk and Guide:
He is telling the story of the Greek King Dionysus

who became master of all India about 2,000 years ago. Dionysus introduced laws, agriculture and left a dynasty of Greek Kings that transferred their power to noble Indians. The Aryan civilization which encountered the Dravidians or native Indians built numerous kingdoms which are no more.
The Indus Valley has ruins which confirm his story at ancient but extinct cities such as Harappa, Mohenjodaro, Kalibangan, Chanludaro and Dhoraji in Gujerat.

The old Buddhist begins to sing the *Samhita hymns*, describing the Indo-Europeans who conquered India over 2000 years ago.

Menander:
What's he singing?

Buddhist Monk:
He is singing the *Samhita hymns*, which describe the Indo-European invasion of India. Then a long process of conquest, assimilation and acculturation began between the two civilizations. Quite fruitful.

Menander, his party and their Buddhist guide approach Atranjikhera city, on the river Ganges, population about 200,000. On landing near a Buddhist compound, they are met by none other than the Venerable Nagasena who embraces Menander and leads his party into the compound.

>Menander:
>Venerable Nagasena, I thank you for the network
>of guides through hostile country.

The Venerable Nagasena leads Menander and his party to a table full of vegetarian food. Menander's advisers lick their lips as they stare at a feast for their eyes. Devamantiya, Anantakaya, Makura and Sabbadina enjoy Chapatti or Flat Whole Wheat Bread with mushroom cream soup. Dosas or Rice Crepes. Sookhi Gobi or Dry Cauliflower. With Shahi Panner and Mattar Paneer or Cheese and Peas. With Mixed Dal or dried beans.

BACTRIA, SAKALA CITY.

> Narrator:
> Menander's Council of 500 which includes the House of the Euthydemids, the Greek Military Elite and Governors of his provinces and sub-kings convene a secret meeting. A Spy in the Secret Service of the Emperor Pushyamitra I was caught trying to enter a forbidden compound, the meeting place of Menander's Council of 500.

> Sub-King Agathocles:
> I am King Agathocles. Who have you caught?

> Greek Guard:
> This man claims to be a merchant from Delhi, but one of our men, has spotted him speaking to the Emperor Pushyamitra in Pataliputra.

The spy is brought before Menander's Council of 500. The spy strains to see the Council, who are seated on the opposite side of a huge underground chamber.

> Sub-King Pantaleon:
> Inhale this agent five times.

The Emperor's spy inhales a hallucinogenic agent and Menander's Council of 500 put on masks from Greek tragedy. Happy, sad, hopeful, despondent, terrified, overjoyed etc. The spy is brought closer to the Council of 500 and stares in horror at the kaleidoscope of faces before him.

        Sub-King Agathocles:
What is your name and rank?

        The Emperor's Spy:
If I tell you, the Emperor will kill my family.

        Sub-King Pantaleon:
We know that your name is Gora Kalla of Vidisa city.

The spy looks at the kaleidoscope of Greek masks before him and struggles to keep sane.

        Sub-King Agathocles:
What is your mission in Sakala city Gora Kalla of Vidisa city?

        Gora Kalla Spy:
The Emperor is anxious to receive all reports relating to the activities of General Menander.

The Council of 500 get up wearing their masks and approach Gora Kalla from Vidisa city and begin to chant "Zeus, Lightning, Thunder, The Furies shall consume you". Gora Kalla is tied to a chair and spun around and faces a large painting of the Olympian god Zeus, throwing a thunder bolt. A tiger enter's and the chamber wall comes down. The spy Gora Kalla faces a tiger, with a look of terror. The hellish screams of the Emperor's spy are heard throughout the corridors of power in Menander's Palace.

PATALIPUTRA, CAPITAL OF THE MAGADHAN EMPIRE.

Emperor Pushyamitra Sunga I is sitting on his peacock throne, with Royal Bodyguards, Greek women guarding the Indian ruler, while he surveys his court. The Chief Military Adviser enters to report on General Menander's activities.

        Emperor Pushyamitra I:
        What are the latest reports on Menander's activities?

        Chief of Military Adviser:
        Menander was last seen heading for Atranjikhera city.

        Emperor Pushyamitra I:
        Menander is an excellent general. But he is a mouse facing an elephant. The Bactrian Greek is outnumbered and outmatched. For 1,000 years 16 Kingdoms have ruled India. Each kingdom ruled by an Indian ruler. India belongs to Indians.

A Buddhist monk dressed as a Brahmin priest begins to laugh out loud. The monk's laughter echoes throughout the Emperor's Palace. Peacocks stretch their colourful tails in the courtyards. The Emperor's Royal Bodyguards comprising Greek women, stare at each other. Emperor Pushyamitra I, angry and now furious, issues orders.

Emperor Pushyamitra I:

Find me the one who is laughing at the Emperor.

Bring him to me. Bring him to me now!!!!

The Emperor's Royal Bodyguards search the Palace and courtyards without locating the culprit.

ATRANJIKHERA CITY, GANGES RIVER, NORTH-WEST OF THE CAPITAL, PATALIPUTRA.

Buddhist monks strike the bronze gongs repeatedly. The Venerable Nagasena and Menander converse in private on the nature of existence.

>Venerable Nagasena:
>Previous effort and present endeavour is what you or your house have achieved and present endeavour is what you, must accomplish.

>Menander:
>Reverend Nagasena, what is the mark of applied thought?

>Venerable Nagasena:
>Fixing the mind sire, on what works, or what matters, is the mark of applied thought.

>Menander:
>Reverend Nagasena, what is the mark of sustained thought?

>Venerable Nagasena:
>As, sire, a bronze gong that has been struck reverberates afterwards and the sound lingers on,

even so, sire, applied thought is to be understood
as striking and sustained thought is to be understood
as reverberating. Keep striking the gong. Banish all
futile thoughts.

MATHURA CITY, NORTH-WEST OF THE CAPITAL, PATALIPUTRA.

Menander and his four advisers enter Mathura city, the birthplace of Krishna, the city of temples. A *Kirtana* performance is underway and the lead singer and instrumentalists achieve osmosis, singing the most ancient *Samhita Hymns*:

> Lead Singer of the Kirtan Performance:
> Let us meditate on that excellent glory of the divine Light. May he inspire our thoughts', and stimulate understandings.[9]

> Devamantiya:
> General, Atranjikhera city has 500 elephants and a cavalry of 50,000. Mathura city has 500 elephants and an infantry of 50,000.

> Menander:
> I want all maps updated for each region we cover. Devamantiya, provide me with a list of elephants, horses, chariots, infantry, and cavalry for each province.

Anantakaya, enters.

---

[9] Edward F. Crangle, *The Origin and Development of Early Indian Contemplative Practices*, (Verlag: Otto Harrassowitz, 1994): 124.

Menander:

Anantakaya, provide me with a list of border towns with strong ramparts. The Emperor's store keepers in each province. And number of superintendents of cities.

Makura enters.

Menander:

Makura, provide me with a list of hostile kings, adversaries or opponents of the Emperor. The number of moats dug. The number of ramparts raised. The number of city gateways built for each city we travel to.

Sabbadina enters.

Menander:

Sabbadina, provide me with the number of grain held in each city we cover.

Menander's four advisers bow and take their leave of the general. The Venerable Nagasena and Menander step out to the balcony and view Mathura city lit up like a thousand candles in the night sky.

Venerable Nagasena:

The heart of India are the five great rivers.

The Ganges, Jumna, Arciravati, Sarabhu and Mahi.

Menander:

A mighty heart. Mark my words, India shall

become the largest democracy in the world.

Let us hope its leaders serve the people and

not themselves.

Venerable Nagasena:

Sire. You are also the heart of India and its future.

THE EMPEROR'S SPIES SEARCH FOR MENANDER'S PARTY IN MATHURA CITY.

The Emperor's son Crown Prince Agnimitra arrives in Mathura city. He is approached by a representative of the Brahminic Faction, named Vishnu.

>Vishnu:
>Welcome Crown Prince, How's the Emperor faring?

>Crown Prince Agnimitra:
>Forget the pleasantries Vishnu. Where are the Bactrian Greeks?

>Vishnu:
>A Brahmin who belong to the Emperor's faction reported seeing a tall and handsome Greek with a party of 9, in the thick and dense forest behind you.

Crown Prince Agnimitra, growing angry.

>Crown Prince Agnimitra:
>Where are they now?

Vishnu:

They disappeared in the market square.

Crown Prince Agnimitra and his security force of deadly Mauryan units marches off to the city-square.

MATHURA CITY. THE FESTIVAL OF DIWALI.

Menander and his four closest advisers along with the Venerable Nagasena and a group of ten Buddhist followers dressed as Brahmin priests walk passed the famous five Brahmanical temples, and twenty Buddhist monasteries. A member of the Buddhist Order approaches the Venerable Nagasena.

> Buddhist Monk Mathura city:
> Venerable Nagasena, The Crown Prince is searching for general Menander and his party.

Suddenly, the singing of *Hare Krishna* pervades the air, as a group of Krishna devotee's beat their drums and sing in different keys, the glory of Krishna's name. The Venerable Nagasena pulls Menander's shirt, telling him to follow him and enter a Buddhist safe house. They come out on to the main street dressed as rich merchants, with coloured beards. Crown Prince Agnimitra scrutinizes the crowd below, searching for any Bactrian Greeks. Suddenly, he sees a tall and handsome merchant with a coloured beard. Menander has spotted him and pretends not to notice him. Crown Prince Agnimitra takes a closer look at the tall rich merchant.

> Crown Prince Agnimitra:
> That's Menander, the Bactrian Greek King.
> Go now. Capture him.

His men race out of the top balcony and down the flight of steps down to the main street. A Buddhist monk races to the Venerable Nagasena to inform him that they have been spotted. Nagasena is seen talking to the main organizer for the *Festival of Diwali*. Crown Prince Agnimitra and his men spot the rich merchants across the road. Suddenly, a large group of devotees block their path as they sing in different keys, the glory of Krishna's name. Crown Prince Agnimitra and his men struggle to cross the path of devotees, but are physically picked up by powerful Indians who are sympathetic to the persecuted Buddhist Order and carried down the street. Menander and his advisers laugh as the spectacle of the Emperor's Chief Security Officer and his men thwarted. The wealthy Greek Merchant observes Menander.

DELHI CITY, NORTH-CENTRAL INDIA.

The Venerable Nagasena and Menander's party arrive in Delhi to see Buddhist temples and compounds up in flames.

>Menander:
>The Emperor's hand has reached Delhi.

The Venerable Nagasena, looks on at the burning compound where he chanted sacred hymns to the glory of Buddha. Tears stream down his face, which a mask of determination and great mental training. Menander's advisers approach him.

>Devamantiya:
>Sire. Delhi has 1,000 elephants and an infantry of 100,000. Half a loyal to the Emperor.

>Anatakaya:
>Sire. Delhi also has 10,000 store-keepers.

>Makura:
>Sire. Delhi also has 40,000 chariots.

>Sabbadina:
>Sire. The number of moats dug and ramparts raised are in my report.

He hands Menander the report. The Venerable Nagasena and Menander's party enter a Buddhist Monastery and burn incense for the persecuted Buddhist monks who are no more.

CHIEF MINISTER YAJNASENA OF THE PARTISAN PARTY BELONGING TO THE ASSASSINATED EMPEROR BRIHADRATHRA CONVENES A MEETING IN VIDARBHA, SOUTH-EAST OF THE CAPITAL, PATALIPUTRA.

Chief Minister Yajnasena:
Ministers of Vidarbha, now is not the time to overthrow Emperor Pushyamitra. The Emperor commands an army of 200,000 infantry, with another 200,000 on call.

Chief Minister of Kausambi:
Emperor Pushyamitra has destroyed Buddhist monasteries and killed vastly learned Buddhist Monks. Buddhism is virtually extinct in the north.

Chief Minister of Mathura:
Our forces are 100,000 strong. We're committed to restoring the Empire of Ashoka. Religious freedom must be restored.

Chief Minister of Ahicchatra:
Chief Minister Yajnasena, you did nothing to protect our assassinated Emperor Brihadrathra and won yourself

the rulership of Vidarbha and now independent.
Neither did the esteemed Ministers of Kausambi or
Mathura.

Chief Minister Yajnasena:
Emperor Pushyamitra is too powerful. When the
the time comes, I shall answer for my actions.
But now, is the time for us to pool our resources and
strike a deal with the most powerful ruler in all India.
Menander the Bactrian Greek.

The Indian rulers and Ministers groan and moan at the thought of foreign intervention in Indian affairs. Behind a screen like tapestry of a ferocious tiger, of 10 metres by 8 metres is Vasumitra, the young son of the Crown Prince Agnimitra. He continues to listen to the minister's plot against the Emperor Pushyamitra. He goes down a narrow corridor and enters a secret door in the palace. He exits the palace and rides a horse to the capital, Pataliputra to inform his grandfather, Emperor Pushyamitra. Vasumitra whispers in the Emperor's ear, all that he has heard in Vidarbha. The Emperor's eyebrows go up and down as he plots his enemy's doom.

163 BCE. SAKALA, CAPITAL OF THE BACTRIAN EMPIRE.

>Narrator:
>Menander is crowned King of Bactria following the death of Apollodotus I.

Agathocleia spots her beloved King Menander going toward his bed chamber. She hides herself behind the curtains and whispers.

>Agathocleia:
>Pssst!!!!!

Menander spins around and examines the empty corridor with rich tapestry every 15 feet. He walks down the corridor and examines the richly coloured curtains. He grabs one curtain in an embrace and receives nothing but air. He walks up to the next curtain and embraces that one also with the same result. Frustrated, he looks around in despair for Agathocleia. The Queen appears behind the next curtain and surprises the King with an embrace and a passionate kiss.

>King Menander:
>Agathocleia, my Queen. Did you receive letters from me?

>Queen Agathocleia:
>Letters don't embrace or kiss.

She looks at him lovingly and in heart-ache at not seeing him for so many months.

                    Queen Agathocleia:
            Touch me.

BACTRA, MOTHER OF CITIES, PARADISE OF THE EARTH. THE CULT OF ANAITIS.

King Menander and Queen Agathocleia arrive at Bactra, the mother of cities and proceed to the Temple of the Goddess Anaitis, with cheering thousands on either side of the main road. The King helps his Queen, now pregnant with their first child, out of the chariot. The royal couple approach the famous cult image of the Goddess Anaitis, goddess of fertility. The image of Anaitis, a large stone sculpture of rich Greek and Indian art, sits upright, wearing a golden crown with eight rays of the sun. One hundred stars clad in skins with thirty beavers of the sheen of silver and gold. The Royal couple bow before the image and burn incense.

Outside, Menander's four advisers and 500 Council Men, led by the powerful Bactrian noble-man, Excursus arrive to the cheers of the Bactrian population. King Menander and Queen Agathocleia emerge from the temple of Anaitis. Menander's four advisers and Excursus along with the 500 Councilmen bow in obeisance before the royal couple. The party walks through the famous markets and bazaars of Bactria, modern Balk in central Asia.

> King Menander:
> Excursus, leader of the Council, what have you to report?

> Excursus Leader of the Council:
> Sire. To remove the tyrant and ruthless Emperor,

the Council has pooled its resources. In addition, we have the support of Bactria; Alexandria-Bactra; Eucratideia in Sogdiana; Alexandria-Eschate; Demetrias in Sogdiana; Thera in Sogdiana; Rhoetea in Bactria and Argos in Scythia. Including 70 of the largest towns of Bactria. 40,000 horses; 20,000 chariots; and 100,000 troops. Landowners plan to add more horses; chariots; and elephants. Currently, we only have 200 elephants.

King Menander:
The Emperor has an infantry of 200,000; 40,000 cavalry; and 2,000 elephants.

Excurses Leader of the Council:
How do we close the gap in numbers?

King Menander:
The *Alexander* Tradition.

Excurses is perplexed.

King Menander:
Alexander left between 8-12 military colonies in India, along the Indus River. We must proceed in stages, winning chief ports; rivers; cities and towns

that can contribute additional numbers in elephants; and, troops as required.

Excurses:
Mercenaries.

King Menander:
Mercenaries. I want accurate numbers on all Superintendents of cities who can contribute, additional manpower and supplies.

Excurses nods in approval and leaves to initiate the King's request for additional information. Alexander, the wealthy Greek Merchant observes Menander from a distance as he distributes gold drachmas to the local children.

MENANDER'S CHIEF ENGINEER AND HIS IMPRESSIVE ALGEBRAIC GEOMETRICAL DESIGNS FOR THE PARABOLOIDAL BURNING MIRROR.

Sabbadina approaches Menander.

> Sabbadina:
> Sire. The Chief Engineer has something to show you.

Menander walks to a large underground antechamber which is the operational war room of the King. On the wall are an impressive array of over 50 algebric geometrical designs at the heart of the construction of the paraboloidal burning mirror.

> Chief Engineer:
> Sire. I have constructed all the paraboloidal burning mirrors. I shall bring down the sun.

Menander walks up to the drawings and marvels at the ingenious and boldness of his Chief Engineer.

> Menander:
> You've utilized all the mines which are at full capacity? You've made use of the ruby, turquoize, lapis lazuli, silver and copper mines.

Chief Engineer:

Yes. Sire.

Menander:

Bring down the sun. Let the sun shine throughout India.

The Chief Engineer pulls some levers and a paraboloidal burning mirror harnesses the rays of the sun and burns through thick timber wood. Menander's Council of 500 erupt in cheers.

INLAND MUMBAI (BOMBAY) THE CAVES OF NASIK, JUNNAR AND KARLI. GREEK MERCHANTS DONATE GIFTS TO THE PERSECUTED BUDDHIST ORDER.

Andronicus and Athina, Greek Merchants in pepper arrive at the Cave of Nasik and descend into the cave to donate gifts to the persecuted Buddhist Order. They see a Buddhist monk set on fire and running through the forest, running from the Emperor's security forces, before collapsing on the ground, dead. Emperor Pushyamitra's troops pass over the cave. He motions to his wife to be quiet.

>Andronicus, the Greek Merchant:
>Athina, we must report on the cruel and unjust treatment of Buddhists communities to King Menander.

>Athina:
>How can the governors and superintendents on the Ganges and Yamuna rivers turn a blind eye to the massacre of the Buddhist communities?

>Andronicus, the Greek Merchant:
>Because they live in fear of the Emperor
>All found not following His orders are tortured or executed.

Athina:

Come on. Let's donate to the Buddhist Order and leave for Sakala. We must speak with King Menander.

162 BCE EMPEROR PUSHYAMITRA CELEBRATES 25 YEARS ON THE THRONE OF MAGADHA.

Rajahs from Chechar, Kumrahar, Chirand, Buxar, Rajghat, Lakshagir, Ayodhya, Sohgaura, Sringverpur, Kara, Pratisthanpur, Kausambi, and Pachkhura arrive in pomp and splendour through the main gate to the capital Pataliputra to pay homage to the usurper, Emperor Pushyamitra I at his palace. Peacocks spread their colourful feathers, reflecting the power and splendour of what was once, the mighty Mauryan Empire which spread throughout much of central and northern India. The Emperor, Crown Prince Agnimitra and Prince Vasumitra and the Rajahs are bedecked with diamonds, which come from the great Deccan plateau. Sapphires, topazes, beryls, cat's eyes, moonstones, amethysts, garnets, and pearls from Southern India and Ceylon are also worn. Rubies from Burma. Emeralds from Egypt. Red coral from the Mediterranean and turquoise from Persia and China are also worn. The gem wealth of India gives the Emperor the means to import huge quantities of gold from the Altai Mountains and traders who never disclosed the richest mines of northern-eastern Massagatae country. A Royal Page reads out the list of Rajahs to the Emperor seated on his peacock throne. The jewels of the Rajahs and especially the Emperor reflect the central idea of Hindu philosophers who saw Kings as divine beings, responsible for upholding and protecting *dharma*, the moral order of the universe.

> Royal Page:
>
> We celebrate the 25th Year of the Reign of
> our Emperor Pushyamitra Sunga who rules
> with compassion and the rule of law.

The Greek merchants' turn their eyes in disgust at the Royal Pages' comments, having seen the persecution of Buddhist communities first hand.

> Royal Page:
> The Rajah of Chechar.

The Rajah of Chechar bows to the Emperor and takes his seat.

> Royal Page:
> The Rajah of Kumrahar.

The Rajah of Kumrahar bows to the Emperor and takes his seat.

> Royal Page:
> The Rajah of Buxar.

The Rajah of Buxar bows to the Emperor and takes his seat.

> Royal Page:
> The Rajah of Rajghat.

The Rajah of Rajghat bows to the Emperor and takes his seat.

> Royal Page:
> The Rajah of Lakshagir.

The Rajah of Lakshagir bows to the Emperor and takes his seat.

>Royal Page:
>The Rajah of Kara.

The Rajah of Kara bows to the Emperor and takes his seat.

>Royal Page:
>The Rajah of Pratisthanpur.

The Rajah of Pratishanpur bows to the Emperor and takes his seat.

>Royal Page:
>The Rajah of Bita.

The Rajah of Bita bows to the Emperor and takes his seat. Greek merchants from Barygaza a major trading port in the South-West of India, approach and bow to the Emperor and take their seats. The Emperor surveys the Rajahs and the foreign dignitaries.

>Emperor Pushyamitra Sunga:
>Welcome all Rajahs of India. Welcome also
>to our foreign dignitaries who have travelled
>to the capital. Do any of you wish to speak
>with me. Please, stand before me and speak.

An elderly Greek Merchant gets up and approaches the dais of the Emperor and bows.

> Greek Merchant from Barygaza:
> Emperor Pushyamitra Sunga, congratulations on a splendid reign.

> Emperor Pushymatria Sunga:
> Speak freely.

> Greek Merchant from Barygaza:
> Is anything being done to protect the Buddhist Order that has been persecuted by a Brahmin faction for over two decades now?

All Rajahs and foreign dignitaries turn their gaze on the Emperor to see what his response shall be.

> Emperor Pushyamitra Sunga:
> All my people are precious to me. The Buddhist Order is special to the Emperor. I shall personally deal with the Brahmin faction which persecutes the Buddhists.

The Greek Merchant bows and takes his seat. The Rajahs begin to murmur amongst themselves. A magnificent table of Indian cuisine is spread out before all the Rajahs and foreign dignitaries. Crown Prince Agnimitra and Prince Vasumitra invite the guests to partake of this sumptuous feast.

Indian dancers begin to perform an elaborate choreography of regional dances from South-Central India to the rhythm and sound of cymbals, drums, flutes, lutes and singers. The Rajah of Kausambi speaks with Emperor Pushyamitra about Menander's growing power.

> Rajah of Kausambi:
> Sire. Menander's power is growing.

> Emperor Pushyamtira Sunga:
> I have crushed all enemies. Greek heroes only
> exist in mythology.

> Rajah of Kausambi:
> Sire. Menander identifies himself with lions.
> He thinks that he can conqueror more territories
> in India than Alexander the Great.

> Emperor Pushymatra Sunga:
> Outside his own kingdom, the hunter, becomes
> the hunted. Let Menander try. I will send him in
> pieces back to Olympus. There are no Greek heroes.

The Greek Merchants go to the balcony and enjoy a serene and clear night sky. Below a row of magnificently decorated procession of elephants pass below the balconies of the palace.

> Elderly Greek Merchant of Barygaza:
> Dharma, moral law has not existed in India since this tyrant took the throne.

> Second Greek Merchant of Barygaza:
> All the governors, superintendents of cities and Store Keepers throughout India, who support this tyrant deserve what's coming to them. Menander will avenge the Buddhist Order.

Crown Prince Agnimitra and Prince Vasumitra approach the Greek Merchants on the balcony. The Greek Merchants turn and bow to them.

> Crown Prince Agnimitra:
> Are you enjoying yourselves?

> Elderly Greek Merchant of Barygaza:
> Immensely, Crown Prince.

They all view the magnificent elephant procession below them. Richly decorated wooden and stone structures are seen along the perimeter of the lake within the capital, Pataliputra.

AN ELITE GROUP OF MERCHANTS MEET IN BARYGAZA, A TRADING PORT, SOUTH-WESTERN INDIA.

The Elderly Greek Merchant and his friend enter a well-guarded compound and disappear down a flight of steps. They enter a large ante-chamber full of some of the wealthiest merchants from the known world. Outside a curious local business owner tries to enter the exclusive meeting of elite merchants. Two 7 foot-tall muscular guards bar his entrance.

>Local Business Owner:
>I wish to enter.

The guards examine him closely and look at their list.

>First Guard:
>What is your name?

>Local Business Owner:
>Vishnu of Barygaza city.

The Guard examines his list.

>First Guard:
>Vishnu of Barygaza city, you're not on the list.

> Local Business Owner:
> I am a local business man. I have a right to enter the meeting.

Both guards grab him and throw him into the Arabian sea. Inside the antechamber the wealthiest merchants in the known world begin their deliberations on what changes must be made on the Indian subcontinent.

THE MERCHANT'S GUILD. A POWER ELITE. ITS INFLUENCE ACROSS THE KNOWN WORLD.

A tall guard strains to hear what the merchant's guild are discussing in the meeting in Barygaza port city. Alexander, the wealthiest Greek merchant takes the podium.

> Alexander the Wealthy Merchant:
> Seven Greek cities in India can contribute to the enterprise.

The tall guard strains to hear what the main speaker is saying.

> Alexander the Wealthy Merchant:
> Peucela and Dionysopolis in Gandhara; Bucephala and Iomousa and Nicaea in the Punjab, Demetrias and Theophila in Sind. Control of the spice trade is paramount.

The tall guard strains to hear what the main speaker is saying once more.

> Alexander the Wealthy Merchant:
> Bactria is one vast garden. A land of irrigation, canals, and tributaries. A land of a thousand cities with as many markets and bazaars. Twelve military colonies along

the frontier in the north and down the Indus River are key. The silver mines of the Panjshir valley is being utilized for the completion of the *phoenix* enterprise.

Tall guards in the inner chamber stop another tall guard from entering the inner chamber.

162-150 BCE. MENANDER BEGINS HIS CONQUESTS IN INDIA. BUDDHISTS PRAY FOR LIBERATION FROM THE RUTHLESS EMPEROR PUSHYAMITRA I.

The Venerable Elder Nagasena enters the palace of King Menander in Sakala, in Bactria for an informal talk on the duties of a King.

> King Menander:
> Welcome Venerable Elder Nagasena.

> Venerable Elder Nagasena:
> Greetings Sire.

> King Menander:
> Venerable Nagasena, what are the duties of a king?

> Venerable Elder Nagasena:
> The duty of the King is to do justice.

> King Menander:
> In what spheres in relation to the people?

> Venerable Elder Nagasena:
> In four spheres. Moral. Religious. Social and Political. Sire. There is a symbol known as the *Wheel of the Chakravartin*. A King of the Wheel is one of those

supreme rulers who from time to time appear and change the world. You Sire, are King of the Wheel.

(Source: Anonymous Tibetan Artist, *Tibetan Buddhist Thangka painting of a Mandala* 19th Century Painting, https://commons.wikimedia.org/wiki/File:Mandala_of_the_Six_Chakravartins. Accessed 04042018).

> King Menander:
>
> Venerable Nagasena, my only aim as a Greek King is to restore Ashoka's Empire in India. To accomplish this task, I must remove a tyrant from the throne of Magadha.

> King Menander:
>
> Venerable Nagasena, the monastery of Ghositarama in Kausambi has been touched by the hand of the Emperor.

Nagasena with a wave of his right hand, dismisses the monastery which is in the control of the tyrant, Pushyamitra I.

> Venerable Nagasena:
>
> Destroy it!!!

Nagasena sees the weight of responsibility on Menander's shoulders. To remove a tyrant and his entire infrastructure of governors and superintendents of cities who turn a blind eye to the persecution of the Buddhist Order is on a mammoth scale and requires not just Greeks but Indians to complete.

> Venerable Elder Nagasena:
>
> Sire. Inhale slowly to the count of 10. Hold your breath, to the count of 10. Now, slowly, exhale to the count of 10.

The Venerable Nagasena rises and bows to King Menander who responds likewise. Menander's closest advisers Devamantiya, Anantakaya, Makura and Sabbadina enter and bow to the King. Followed by two Greek Merchants, Andronicus and Athina.

Devamantiya:
Sire. Greek merchants from Mumbai wish to have an audience with you. Andronicus and his wife Athina.

Menander:
Welcome.

Andronicus the Greek Merchant:
Sire, we trade spices up and down the Ganges and Yamuna Rivers. What pains us is the persecution of the Buddhist communities by the Emperor. The parasites along the Ganges and Yamuna Rivers, who call themselves governors, superintendents of cities and store-keepers take half of all the revenue from agriculture and leave the poor farmers with little or nothing.

Athina the Greek Merchant:
Sire. With my own eyes, I have seen Buddhist monks

set on fire by the Emperor's security forces.
Governors, superintendents and shop-keepers all along
the Ganges, Yamuna, Brahmaputra, Son, Sind and
Chambal Rivers are turning a blind eye to the
massacre of the Buddhists.

Tears streaming down her face, she implores the King of Bactria.

Athina the Greek Merchant:
Sire. You have the power, the resources of nine
Greek Provinces in India, and 70 Bactrian
cities who can provide you with all the resources
to put an army together, to remove this tyrant,
Pushyamitra who uses fire to destroy the monasteries.

Menander:
Did you say, *fire*?

Athina nods and looks at the steely eyed, thoughtful King, Menander, who envisions all corridors down the Ganges, Yamuna, Ravi, Son and many more with entire cities on fire. Anantakaya enters with Yajnasena, the Chief Minister of the previous Emperor of Magadha.

Anantakaya:
Sire. Yajnasena, the Chief Minister of the previous

Emperor requests and audience with you.

King Menander signals that the interview with the Greek Merchants from Mumbai has concluded and indicates with a gesture of his right hand, that they can leave now, with they do so. Menander rises to greet the Chief Minister of the previous Emperor.

>Menander:
>Chief Minister Yajnasena, I last saw you when
>I was just a young man.

>Yajnasena, Chief Minister of Vidarbha:
>Sire. Now I am an old man and you a King and
>an excellent general.

Menander's closest advisers invite the Chief Minister to a table with some of the finest meals in Bactria.

>Yajnasena, Chief Minister of Vidarbha:
>Ministers of Emperor Brihadathra are not pleased
>with the extermination policy of Emperor
>Pushyamitra, against the Buddhist Order. If you march
>on the capital, Pataliputra, we shall support you in the
>south. We seek a return to Dhamma, law and religious
>freedom for the people.

Menander:
Ashoka's Empire and restoration of his 14 edicts.[10]

Yajnasena, Chief Minister of Vidarbha:
Emperor Pushyamitra is determined to wipe out the Buddhist Order. He is bent, on promoting the caste system throughout the Empire. Lower castes who perform menial jobs must keep a distance from the upper castes. Lower castes are not allowed to to use the same bathing tanks or draw drinking water from the same wells. The caste system is discriminatory, rigid and pernicious.

Menander:
Buddhism shall rise from the ashes and blossom and grow once more.

The Chief Minister nods his approval of King Menander's solution.

---

[10] Ven. S. Dhammika, *The Edicts of King Ashoka*, Kandy: Buddhist Publication Society, 1993.

THE CASTE SYSTEM IN DELHI. THE BRAHMIN RELIGIOUS POLICE.

In Delhi city, a farmer and his fifteen-year old daughter approach a well, guarded by Brahmin religious police. The farmer notices the Brahmin police looking away. He goes to draw water. The Brahmin religious police strike him with their long thick sticks on the head. The farmer fall's, down, with blood streaming down his face. With tears in her eyes, the farmer's daughter runs to help her father to his feet. She addresses the Brahmins.

> Farmer's Daughter:
> My father is deaf and dumb. All he wants is to drink some water.

The Brahmin religious police look at the farmer with contempt and ask.

> Brahmin Religious Police:
> What is your father's profession?

> Second Brahmin Religious Police:
> What is your father's title?

> Farmer's Daughter:
> We're farmers.

The Brahmin Religious Police escort the farmer and his daughter outside the compound.

Brahmin Religious Police:
This well is reserved for merchants, Brahmins,
Store Keepers and the Governor. Move on.

The farmer and his daughter make their way to the main road. A Buddhist monk approaches them and escorts them to the monastery. He dresses the wounds of the farmer and serves a warm meal and supplies them with all the water they require. The farmer's daughter tries to touch the feet of the Buddhist monk, who refuses but helps her up and gives her a basket of food to take on her journey.

CROWN PRINCE AGNIMITRA AND HIS SON VASUMITRA ORGANIZE FIFTEEN CITIES TO ATTACK MENANDER'S APPROACH TO THE CAPITAL DOWN THE PRINCIPAL RIVERS, THE GANGES AND THE JUMNA RIVERS.

Crown Prince Agnimitra and his son Vasumitra approach the Ganges River to speak to Military Commanders.

>Crown Prince Agnimitra:
>Commander, I want all the principal governors, Superintendents of cities, the Emperor's Store Keepers to destroy Menander's fleet as they advance down the Ganges and Jumna Rivers. Is that understood?

>Unit Commander:
>Yes, Crown Prince.

>Crown Prince Agnimitra:
>Alert the governors and superintendents of cities on the Indus, Chambal, Sindhu, Narmada, Son, Ghaghara and Ravi rivers to attack all transports belonging to Menander.

Vasumitra runs up to his brother, the Crown Prince and looks the Unit Commander in the eye.

Prince Vasumitra:

Menander must not be allowed to penetrate the capital, Pataliputra.

The Unit Commander nods affirmatively and exits.

THE EMPEROR'S HAND. FIFTEEN CITIES AND OVER 10 RIVERS ARE PREPARING TO ATTACK MENANDER'S ADVANCE SOUTH TO THE CAPITAL, PATALIPUTRA.

Prince Vasumitra shouts orders to governors on the Ganges River to prepare for Menander's attack.

                Prince Vasumitra:
        Prepare the Ganges River for Menander's attack.

Villagers hurry to prepare for Menander's attack, storing weapons along the river. Crown Prince Agnimitra inspects the Jumna River and issues orders to the governors.

                Crown Prince Agnimitra:
        Prepare the Jumna River for Menander's attack.

Moats are dug and ramparts are raised at Atranjikhera, Sringverpur, Jhunsi, Lakshagir, Ayodhya, Sohagavra, Varanasi, Buxar Chirand, Pataliputra, Ujjain to Sohagaura nearly 800 kilometres from south to north. Delhi, Hastinapur, Mathura to Pataliputra and Chechar about 800 kilometres from west to east.

169-150 BCE. MENANDER'S WAR COUNCIL AND CONQUESTS IN INDIA.

Menander, followed by his four closest advisers, Devamantiya, Anantakaya, Makura and Sabbadina pass a corridor depicting paintings of *Heracles and his Twelve Labours*; *The Twelve Olympian Gods in the Throne Room of the Gods on Mt. Olympus*; *Alexander and Rajah Porus at the Battle of the Hyphasis River*; and a large painting of *Zeus throwing a Thunderbolt from Mt. Olympus*. They enter the War Council of Bactria and face 500 Councilmen from all Provinces of the Bactrian-Greek Empire.

> King Menander:
> The Emperor Pushyamitra Sunga has wiped out the Buddhist communities in the north-east. He has invaded our territory once before. He rose to the throne of the Mauryan Empire through violence and terror. I, Menander the Protector, shall remove him with thunder and lightning.

The 500 Councilmen rise and applaud the King for the stance he is taking against the usurper, Emperor Pushyamitra I.

> King Menander:
> Intelligence reports on the 118 Indian tribes on the 58 rivers of India who are loyal to the Emperor and those who oppose him

are known to us. We shall shut down all war material reaching the capital Pataliputra. The Ganges, Jumna, Ravi, Son, Indus, and Chenab Rivers shall be taken by us. Make no mistake, the Emperor is going to un-leash all his fury at the Indo-Greek army coming for him. On the next full moon, I Menander Soter, shall invade.

The 500 Councilmen stand up and applaud the King.

Narrator:
Menander's sub-kings Epander and Polyxenus lead naval units on the Ganges and Jumna Rivers.

Sub-King Epander:
Steady as she goes.

He looks up at the starry night sky.

Sub-King Epander:
Orion's Belt. Kausambi is behind us.

The eerie silence is broken by the sound of war drums. A musician in Epanders' unit alerts the King.

Naval Officer:

Epander, Sire. The sound of drums is a warning. The Emperor's hand has reached this region.

Sub-King Epander looks out at the lights of the villagers on the shore. Suddenly, a flotilla of boats is attacked by a volley of arrows which strike almost every part of the flotilla of ships.

Sub-King Epander:

It's an attack. Hit the deck.

A shower of arrows, strike Indo-Greek naval officers who fall overboard. Epander helps a wounded soldier down below. He comes back out and issues orders.

Sub-King Epander:

Fire!!!!!!!!

Epander's flotilla of boats fires a large volley of arrows at the villagers on the shore. His ship lands on the shore, not far from the enemy camp. His men disembark and attack the enemy strong hold. A furious exchange of swords and fighting ensues between Epanders' naval officers and forces loyal to the Emperor of Magadha. Epanders' forces are overwhelmed when Menander arrives with his large force and defeats the enemy stronghold.

SUB-KING POLYXENUS'S NAVAL OPERATIONS ON THE JUMNA RIVER.

Sub-King Polyxenus's flotilla of boats goes down the Jumna River. The eerie silence is unnerving to only a few of the soldiers. A naval officer approaches Polyxenus.

> Naval Officer:
> Polyxenus, Sire. The cities of Bucephala on the Jhelum, Alexandria, Iomousa in Upper Chenab, Calliope, Asterosia, Daedala, Iocates and Tyre have contributed supplies.

Sub-King Polyxenus looks up at the starry night sky.

> Sub-King Polyxenus:
> The constellation Leo. Steady as she goes.

The sound of war drums is heard on the distant shore. The sound and beat or rhythm increases to a feverish pitch. Suddenly, Polyxenus's flotilla of boats is attacked by a volley of arrows. Scores of Indo-Greek soldiers are struck and wounded and some killed.

> Sub-King Polyxenus:
> Hit the deck.

Sub-King Polyxenus runs to the commander of his units.

Sub-King Polyxenus:
Fire on that position on the shore. Fire!!!

A large volley of arrows hits the shore and many of the enemy loyal to the Emperor are struck and killed or wounded. Polyxenus lands his ship not far from the enemy camp and attacks it with a concentrated cavalry charge.

EXCURGUS.'S NAVAL OPERATIONS ON THE INDUS RIVER.

Excurgus, leader of the Council of 500 in Menander's Court, leads war supplies down the Indus river, destined for the main trading port of Barygaza, a Greek city in south-western India.

>Excurgus:
>
>We must get this shipment to Menander for his final assault on the capital.

>Naval Officer:
>
>Excurgus, drums are being struck down river.

Excurgus strains his ear, and hear the sound of drums on the far shore. He looks up at the night sky.

>Excurgus:
>
>The constellation Hydra. Steady as she goes.
>
>Keep me informed if the drums …

Before he can finish his sentence, a large volley of arrows hit the flotilla of boats transporting material for Menander's final assault.

>Excurgus:
>
>Hit the deck.

Arrows hit all parts of the flotilla. Excurgus signals a full assault on the enemy camp on the far shore. He points to the far shore.

<blockquote>
Excurgus:

Fire.
</blockquote>

A large volley of iron tipped arrows flies towards the enemy camp and the Emperor's supporters are hit and killed.

150 BCE. EMPEROR PUSHYAMITRA SUNGA'S WAR COUNCIL, THE CAPITAL, PATALIPUTRA CITY, GANGES VALLEY.

One hundred Rajas are seated in the main palace. Emperor Pushyamtra Sunga enters and sits on his throne. Crown Prince Agnimitra and his son Vasumitra sit next to the Emperor. Advance scouts of the Emperor arrive to report on Menander's invasion.

>Emperor Pushyamitra Sunga:
>What are the latest intelligence reports on Menander's movements?

>Advance Scout:
>Sire. We anticipated the populations of the 15 cities on the Ganges and Jumna Rivers estimated at 1.5 million loyal to the House of Magadha, to resist Menander.

>Emperor Pushyamitra Sunga:
>And have they resisted the invader?

>Advance Scout:
>Sire. Menander is using a strange blinding light, and has conquered all fifteen cities and four main fortresses. Governors, Superintendents of cities and Store Keepers

loyal to the Emperor have perished.

Emperor Pushyamitra Sunga reads out the list with growing impatience and anger.

>Emperor Pushyamitra Sunga:
>Kausambi, Bhita, Jhusi, Mathura, Purana Qila, Hastinapur, Atranjikhera, Sringverpur, Lakshagir, Ayodhya, Sohagaura, Rajghat, Buxar, Chirand, Checkar and Dangawara. Now the capital, Pataliputra is threatened.

>Advance Scout:
>Sire. Menander strikes with a furious volley of eight different type of iron tipped arrows. Followed by 40 siege engines which catapult wooden balls of fire, weighing over 500 kilograms which destroy all city walls. The dust from Menander's marching army blocks the sun.

>Emperor Pushyamitra Sunga:
>Does Menander possess an army of 200,000?

>Advance Scout:
>Over 200,000. And over 2,000 elephants.

Emperor Pushyamitra Sunga:
Prepare the capital for a prolonged siege. Man the towers. Prepare to fire all our weapons on Menander.

The Emperor looks to his son, Crown Prince Agnimitra and grandson Vasumitra and his Chief Military Advisers.

Emperor Pushyamtra Sunga:
Crown Prince Agnimitra and grandson Vasumitra, prepare all 570 towers for defence. Set on fire, anyone who tries to cross the main ditch dug around the perimeter of the capital. Reinforce all 64 gates to defend the capital. To my military commanders deploy our 2,000 elephants to defend the perimeter of the city. Deploy our 200,000 troops to defend the capital. Recall all further troops to defend the capital. Menander shall face the death of a thousand krait snake bites.

169-150 BCE. MENANDER'S CONQUESTS IN INDIA

Narrator:

The death of his three senior contemporaries and principal antagonists, Demetrius, Apollodotus, and Eucratides between 167 BCE and 159 BCE, left Menander the sole master of a vast territory in India, extending from Gandhara to the region of Meerut, Hastinapur and Ahicchatra in Uttar Pradesh. Sindh, Kutch, and Gujarat are now also in his possession. Menander's swiftness, speed and surprise help him conquer the following cities: Cartana, Ghazni, Gandhara, Jalalabad, Sakala, Jlandhar, Sonipat, Hastinapur, Delhi, Atranjikhera, Bairat, Mathura, Ahicchatra, Sohgaura, Ayodhya, Chirand, Chechar, Kumrahar, Buxar, Raighat, Lakshagir, Sringverpur, Kara, Pratishthanpur, the fortress of Kausambi the most populous city of Madhyadesa. Paachkhura and Kara also fall.

MENANDER DEFEATS THE POWERFUL FEUDATORY KINGS OF MATHURA AND PANCHALA, FACTIONS LOYAL TO THE EMPEROR, WHO JOIN FORCES WITH MENANDER.

The powerful feudatory kings of Mathura and Panchala approach Menander, after an epic battle lasting 72 hours. Menander's use of eight type of iron-tipped arrows, catapult artillery, both the sling shot and crossbow types. Capable of hurling 500-kilogram missiles of fire and the blinding light of the burning mirrors convince the powerful kings of Mathura and Panchala that Menander has God on his side.

> The King of Mathura:
> Menander, you're the victor. I King of Mathura, join you in your final battle for the capital, Pataliputra.

> The King of Panchala:
> Menander, I King of Panchala, too, acknowledge you as victor. I join you on your final march on the capital to remove the tyrant, Pushyamitra.

All three Kings raise their swords to the heavens and cheers of all the Indo-Greeks resound throughout the area. Menander's four closest advisers, Devamantiya, Anantakaya, Makura and Sabbadina organize the transport of 2,000 elephants; 1,000,000 iron tipped arrows in eight categories; 80,000 chariots and horses; and an Indo-Greek Army of 200,000 and growing.

BUDDHIST MONKS WALK ALONG THE HIGHEST HILLS OF THE CAPITAL PATALIPUTRA AT AN ELEVATION OF 53 METRES.

The Venerable Nagasena leads a long line of Buddhist Monks along a path at a height of 53 metres to view the approaching Indo-Greek Army of Menander I Soter. Buddhist Monks strike the bronze gongs throughout India at the same time. They begin to pray for Menander's success against the usurper and tyrant, Emperor Pushyamitra Sunga I. The Buddhists view a long line of elephants numbering 2,000 passing. Followed by 80,000 chariots, 120,000 horses and an Indo-Greek Army of over 200,000 troops, heading for the capital Pataliputra. The dust from Menander's army blocks the sun, temporarily. Suddenly, 80 massive Siege engines pass the monks view, followed by numerous transports.

Emperor Pushyamitra directs his commanders who command a total force of 200,000 outside the perimeter of the capital. 2,000 elephants surround the capital. The deep ditch dug around the capital appears formidable. Indian archers, expert at aiming a formidable arrow a metre in length and armed with a poisonous iron tip which can pierce any armour known to man is ready for use. 570 towers are stocked with a combined number of arrows at 1 crore or 1 million. The sound of Buddhist horns fills the air with anticipation of epic proportions.

People in the capital of Pataliputra are panic stricken and are seen leaving with all belongings out of the 64 gates, which are ordered closed and locked. Emperor Pushyamitra, Crown

Prince Agnimitra and his son Vasumitra and 100 ministers look out from the balcony at the approaching Indo-Greek Army led by Menander. Chief Minister Yajnasena who leads the Partisan Party advances with an Indian army of 20,000 to his left. The minister intends to maintain his position and not interfere in the conflict. He intends to divert the attention of Emperor Pushyamitra and open two fronts. Leaving Menander enough room to defeat the Emperor's forces. Menander's Indo-Greek Army comes to a stop, outside the imposing walls of the capital, Pataliputra. Facing him, is the Emperor with a row of elephants and an army of 200,000. The steel helmets of the Greeks gleaming in the sun in a row of spectacular military precision and discipline are viewed by the population.

150 BCE. MENANDER INVADES THE CAPITAL OF THE MAURYAN EMPIRE, PATALIPUTRA, 9 MILES LONG, 1.5 MILES WIDE. WITH 570 TOWERS AND 64 GATES. THE FIRST PHASE.

Menander I Soter rides a white horse in front of his Indo-Greek Army. He addresses Emperor Pushyamitra and his army.

> Menander:
> I am Menander I Soter, King of Bactria. I have come to contest the title of Maharajah of Maharajas and Dharmaraja or King of Justice.

Emperor Pushyamitra rides his chariot in front of his Indian Army.

> Emperor Pushyamitra I:
> I am Pushyamitra Sunga, Emperor of India.
> I accept your challenge Menander, King of Bactria.
> A fight, to the death!!!

Drums and cymbals are sounded in the capital, signalling the Emperor's massive launch of missiles on to Menander's Bactrian Greek Army. Menander signals the trumpeters to begin and the signal to the Indo-Greek Army to launch eight different types of iron tipped arrows at the 570 towers and the *mahouts* or drivers of the elephants begins.

Menander spear heads his celebrated Bactrian cavalry and Indo Greek Army to engage the Emperor's forces outside the city walls from the West. His goal is to encircle the capital from the North East. A furious engagement between the Indo-Greek army and the Emperor's army ensues outside the main gate to the capital. Menander's Engineering Units deploy 570 burning mirrors and 64 larger burning mirrors focussed on the towers and wooden gates.

The sun overhead is harnessed and the paraboloidal burning mirrors concentrate the sun's rays into deadly rays which begin to set on fire, each tower, each gate. Menander assaults the front or main gate of the capital with his catapult artillery units who hurl a volley of 500- kilogram balls of fire create a breach on the massive gate. Boiling water is poured on to the Greek army from the towers. The Greeks respond in a furious eight -pronged assault, with eight different types of iron tipped arrows, targeting the attackers on the walls of the capital.

Menander's siege engines target the 570 towers of the capital in systematic fashion. Emperor Pushyamitra directs the elephants to concentrate into a massive wall and attacks Menander's infantry. Menander directs his infantry to separate columns and avoids the brunt of the massive attack of elephants. Some Greek soldiers are crushed by the elephants. Menander directs his elephants to concentrate on the right wing of the Emperor's infantry and the elephants rush into a collision with the finest soldiers fighting under the Emperor and many are crushed or injured in the assault. The Emperor directs the Indian archers on the 570 towers to begin a massive second volley of large arrows to be shot at the Greek army.

Scores of Greek soldiers are killed or injured. Menander directs his second volley of iron tipped arrows which are shot at the attackers on the 570 towers. Menander directs a second volley of siege engines to fire a volley of 500-kilogram missiles at the Eastern gates, causing massive fires and destruction. The Bactrian cavalry ride into the Emperor's infantry positioned on the Eastern side, guarding the subsidiary and main gates. A furious exchange of swords ensues between the combatants.

Crown Prince Agnimitra and his son Vasumitra engage the Greek forces on the Northern subsidiary and main gates to the capital. Devamantiya leads a squadron of Indo-Greek infantry to engage the Crown Prince Agnimitra and his son Vasumitra, gaining the upper hand. Emperor Pushyamitra leads a main body of Indian infantry to engage Menander's left flank. The Emperor is trying to catch Menander in a pincer movement. Menander anticipates this, and attacks the Emperor's right wing with full force, breaking through and forcing the Emperor to withdraw from his position. Anantakaya order a third wave of iron tipped arrows to be fired at the remaining attackers on the 570 towers with devastating results. The Emperor directs another elephant assault on Menander, who meets him head on.

EMPEROR PUSHYAMITRA'S REINFORCEMENTS FROM TERRITORIES FURTHER EAST COME DOWN FROM THE BRAHMAPUTRA RIVER.

Ten divisions made up of 20,000 infantry troops arrive at the capital, Pataliputra. They engage Menander's forces from the north-east; and north west. At the same time, in which Menander's forces appear to be surrounded, Sub-Kings Polyexenus and Epander arrive from the Ganges and Jumna Rivers and engage the Emperor's reinforcements in furious hand to hand combat. Crown Prince Agnimitra directs an infantry of 20,000 on Menander's right wing. Menander directs his siege engine closest to him to direct a volley of missiles on to the enemy line with devastating results.

                Menander:

           Fire.

Menander then directs the siege engines in front of the main gate of the capital to catapult a concentrated bombardment 500- kilogram fire balls which damage the reinforced timber door and cause the first breach or crack in the massive gate. Prince

                Menander:

           Fire.

Vasumitra directs a line of elephants against Menander's main force which temporarily delays the catapult assault on the main gate.

Prince Vasumitra:

Attack.

Menander directs a pincer movement on Prince Vasumitra, who realizes what is about to happen and orders his troops to withdraw to the western gate of the capital and re-group.

Emperor Pushyamitra on his elephant, directs a line of elephants to attack Menander's main force.

Emperor Pushyamitra:

Attack.

The line of elephants under the mahouts or drivers advance on Menander and are met with the crack Cretan archers who fire a volley of all eight types of iron tipped arrows on the drivers. The driverless elephants go on a rampage, crushing both Greek and Indian soldiers.

Menander:

Fire.

Menander directs his siege engines to fire a line of missiles to force the elephants into the main ditch dug around the capital. Menander then summons his chariot drivers to concentrate on the Emperor's main force.

Menander:

Go after the Emperor.

He directs his siege engine unit commanders to fire a concentrated burst of missiles on the Emperor's main group, forcing it, back towards the main gate, north of the capital. The Emperor orders the main gate open, and retreats into the capital and orders the main closed and reinforced. The Emperor begins to see numerous towers on fire. Main gates are also on fire. A blinding light temporarily blinds him, and he withdraws into his palace and prepares for his counter-attack.

THE EMPEROR'S FURY.

All 570 towers are manned up with men, loyal to the death to the Emperor. Troops, with expert archers of the long arrow, which can penetrate any armour known to man. 1,000,000 large arrows are prepared and ready to be deployed. Menander and his four closest advisers notice frantic activity on the north wall towers.

Menander:

Unit Commanders, shields!!!!!

Menander's infantry, cavalry, siege engine unit commanders, mahouts of elephant drivers. Sub-King Epander and Polyxenus. The King of Mathura and Pachala. All men and women shield themselves for the storm of large arrows about to rain down on them. Emperor right hand which temporarily blocks the sun.

Emperor Pushyamtra:

Fire!!!!!!!!!!!!!

THE EMPEROR RAINS DOWN THOUSANDS OF IRON-TIPPED HEAVY ARROWS ON TO THE INDO-GREEK ARMY, WHICH ADAPTS AND IMPROVES.

Expert Indian archers systematically fire their heavy arrows on Menander's elephants, infantry, chariots and cavalry with negligible results. In a prearranged move, Menander orders his troops to divide into small units and to become mobile with locked shields. The Emperor on his balcony observes the strangest manoeuvres he has ever encountered on the battlefield. Menander's forces transform into dyad formations; triad formations; tetrad formations; pentad formations; hexad formations; heptad formations; octad formations; ennead formations; and decad formation. The Emperor's expert archers are having a difficult time aiming their heavy arrows at Menander's moving targets. Now, the Emperor observes another strange manoeuvre by Menander's units. Fire battle formation equals 24 right angled triangles, surrounded by four equilaterals, and each equilateral consists of 6 right angled triangles.

Emperor Pushyamitra Sunga:

Fire!!!

Air battle formation equals 48 triangles, surrounded by 8 equilaterals, octahedron surrounded by 8 equilateral traingles, each of which is separated into 6 right angled triangles become 48 in all.

Emperor Pushyamitra Sunga:

Fire!!!

Water battle formation equals 120 triangles, surrounded by 20 equilaterals, similar to an icosahedron, which is composed of 120 equilateral triangles.

>Emperor Pushymitra Sunga:
>
>Fire!!!

Either battle formation equals 12 equilateral pentagons, a dodecahedron.

>Emperor Pushyamitra Sunga:
>
>Fire!!!

And Earth battle formation equals 48 triangles surrounded by 6 equilateral tetragons, a cube. The cube is surrounded by 6 tetragons, each of which is separated into 8 triangles, so that they become 48 in all.

>Emperor Pushyamitra Sunga:
>
>Fire!!!

Emperor Pushyamitra Sunga is frustrated and orders his unit commanders to keep firing missiles on Menander's mobile army.

MENANDER'S FURY. THE INDO-GREEK INVASION OF THE MAGADHAN CAPITAL PATALIPUTRA.

Menander and his four closest advisers meet to plan the final phase of the attack on the capital. An Indian archer spots Menander and takes aim. He fires and the meter long, iron-tipped - arrow is on target.

> Menander:
> I want the Spring-powered artillery units to destroy the moats around the perimeter of the capital. The catapults to take out the towers. The mobile ramps to smash down the gates to the capital. Then, storm the capital.

The Indian archer has fired his meter- long arrow and it strikes Menander in the head. Menander falls to the ground from the force of the blow. The steel helmet Menander is wearing has saved his life. A superficial cut down the side of his left forehead causes blood to stream down the side of his face. Menander's four advisers, believing that the king is dead, issue Menander's final instructions to the engineering units. Menander's engineers go into full gear, concentrating all their fire power and 500- kilogram missiles on the 570 towers and 64 gates. Menander's original instructions circumnavigate the entire Indo-Greek force, positioned around the 9 -mile by 1.5- mile diameter of the capital.

Excurgus, Leader of the Council of 500 Bactrian Greeks arrives with his transports full of 500- kilogram missiles destined for the Engineering Units. He is approached by Makura.

Makura:
Menander is dead. The King's final instructions …

Makura points to the huge walls of the capital. Excurgus, enraged, transports the war material and the engineers systematically destroy the moats, towers, gates and storm the capital via the main gate, which has been smashed to pieces by the sustained bombardment from the catapults.

Menander awakens from being temporarily knocked out. He insists on getting up himself, and wipes off the cake of blood on his right cheek.

Sabbadina:
Sire. We've destroyed the towers and gates. The capital, Pataliputra, is ours!!!!

Menander and his four closest advisers ride in four horse chariots into the capital, emerging from the dust and devastation around them. The Indo-Greek Army enters the capital and seeks out any of the Emperor's troops. The right side of Menander's face appears marble like, from the white dust which has covered the blood, streaming down his face.

EMPEROR PUSHYAMITRA ESCAPES THE CAPITAL.

The Maharajah observes from his western balcony, Yasjasena, Chief Minister for the Partisan Party from Vidarsa. He raises his right fist in the air.

Emperor Pushyamitra Sunga:
Traitor!!!!

He goes to the northern balcony. Emperor Pushyamitra Sunga now observes Menander riding into the capital. In horror, he views the 9- mile huge walls of timber and mud on fire. Numerous towers are also on fire. With no time to lose, he goes into another room and lies down on an 8 x 5meter carpet. His loyal attendants roll him up into a carpet, destined for transport outside the capital. His attendants, dressed as Buddhist Monks carry the Emperor, concealed in the carpet, out of the palace. Menander, his four closest advisers and Personal Bodyguards escort the new Maharajah to his throne. Makura notices the four Buddhist Monks carrying the carpet out of the palace.

Makura:
Stop. Where are you taking the carpet?

The Emperor tries his best not to breath or make a sound, inside the carpet. Menander goes up to the carpet and taps it with his sword.

False Buddhist Monk:
To the local monastery.

Menander's eyes narrow as he visualizes the persecuted Buddhist monks in his mind.

Menander:
Let them go.

The imposters posing as Buddhist monks bow and take their leave. The Emperor is transported to modern Orissa, further east.

MAHARAJAH OF MAHARAJAHS, DHARMARAJAH, KING OF JUSTICE.

The Emperor's Royal Bodyguards stand to attention. Menander enters the main hall and observes that they are Greek women of fine appearance and bearing. Menander sits on the Mauryan throne and recovers his faculties. Yasjasena, Chief Minister of the Partisan Faction in the Mauryan Empire enters. He brings two prisoners. Crown Prince Agnimitra and Prince Vasumitra.

>Yasjasena, Chief Minister of the Partisan Party:
>Congratulations Sire. You are now, Maharajah of Maharajas and Dharmarajah, King of Justice. You have restored Dhamma.

>Menander:
>No Minister. I am not the Emperor of India.

The Crown Prince Agnimitra and his son Prince Vasumitra are brought before Menander.

>Menander:
>You fought well, Crown Prince.

>Crown Prince Agnimitra:
>Sire. You are the victor.

Menander:
Vasumitra, you showed great valour.

Prince Vasumitra;
Sire. You are the victor.

Yasjasena, Chief Minister of the Partisan Party:
Sire. Leave them to me.

All three men bow to Menander and take their leave. Menander, still bleeding from the superficial wound to his forehead, approaches the balcony on the north to address the people of the capital and his Indo-Greek army.

Menander:
I, Menander I Soter, King of the Bactrian Greeks,
am Your Protector. Dharma, law is restored.

The Indo-Greek Army shouts in unison, the following that would be etched in stone, for a future archaeologist to discover and local villagers to worship. The Indians chant first in Pakrit, an Indian dialect infused with Sanskrit words:

The Indo-Greek Army:
maharajasa rajarajasa
mahamtasa tratarasa dhammi
kasa jayamtasa ca apra

jitasa Minanada de rasa.

Now, the Greek soldiers chant in Attic Greek:

        The Indo-Greek Army:
        BASILEOS BASILEON
        MEGALOU SOTEROS
        DIKAIOU NIKETOROU KAI ANIKETOU
        MENANDROU

On Screen: King of Kings
                        Great Protector!
                        Righteous Victor and Invincible
                        Menander.

150 BCE MENANDER'S ACTS OF PIETY AS THE NEW MAHARAJA OF MAHARAJAS AND DHARMARAJAH, KING OF JUSTICE OF INDIA.

Menander's entourage is escorted on to the main park and man-made lakes of the palace complex of the Mauryan Empire. He steps off his chariot and is greeted with hundreds of Buddhist monks from the Kukkutarama Monastery. The Monks raise him to their shoulders and carry him along the lake pathway within the palace and capital to the cheers of Buddhist monks who have suffered persecution over a thirty-year period from the usurper and deposed Emperor Pushyamitra Sunga. The joy and gratitude on their faces cannot be expressed in words. Only minorities who have suffered genocide or persecution can relate to the truth of the historical events in this story. The Buddhist Monks approach the Venerable Elder Nagasena, who raises his hands to the heavens in gratitude to the All Compassionate Buddha for Menander's supreme sacrifice in wiping out the old and corrupt political and religious bureaucracy who allowed the usurper Pushyamitra to continue his persecution of Buddhist monks for thirty years. Menander bows before the Venerable Nagasena and following custom touches his feet. The Venerable Nagasena, helps him to his feet and embraces him as they smile at the incredible events which have unfolded and freed the Buddhist communities throughout India. Sabbadina approaches Menander with a group of Greek merchants.

Sabbadina:
Sire. The merchants wish to know if they can trade.

Menander:

Nothing moves in India during my religious obligations. In 30 days, a plan to rebuild India in Ashoka's vision shall commence.

Sabbadina and the merchants bow and take their leave. Menander turns and observes a poor boy of five, raise his hands towards the sky. Just then, the monsoons arrive and rain down on the capital Pataliputra. The boy aged five still has his hands raised to the heavens, and enjoys the sun-shower. The boy wears a priceless look of complete contentment on his face.

On Screen: In 146 BCE deposed Emperor Pushyamitra was killed in a final battle with Menander outside the capital of Bactria, Sakala. In the south, Prince Vasumitra founds the Sunga Dynasty. Menander reigned for 30 years.

King Menander and Queen Agathocleia and their son Strato I view the majestic Himalayas from their palace in Sakala, North India. Below them, the bazaars and markets of Sakala city are full of colour and international traders and buyers. A wealthy Greek Merchant from Alexandria, Ptolemaic Egypt has arrived. He distributes gold drachmas to the children of Sakala city. He requests an audience with the King and is admitted. Menander and Queen Agathocleia finally meet their mysterious benefactor. The most powerful Greek Merchant in the world. The merchant presents the King with a large lion made of solid Gold.

On Screen: Wicked Yavanas (Greeks) conquered the capital,

Pataliputra.

The Yuga Purana.

Milinda is a Prince of Buddhism.

Milinda is a champion of Buddhism.

The Milindapanha.

THE END.

References:

1. P. A. Brunt ed. *Arrian: History of Alexander & Indica*, Cambridge: Harvard University Press, 1983.
2. T.W. Rhys Davies, *The Questions of King Milinda, 2 Vols*. Oxford: Clarendon Press, 1890, 1894.
3. Nalinaksha Dutt, *Buddhist Sects in India*, Delhi, Motilal Banarsidass, 1978.
4. Etienne Lamotte, *History of Indian Buddhism*, Louvain, Paris: Peeters Press, 1988.
5. B.C. Law, *A History of Pali Literature Vol. II*. London: Kegan Paul, Trench, Trubner, 1933.
6. V. D. Mahajan, *Ancient India*, New Delhi: S. Chand Press, 1960.
7. V. S. Misra, *Ancient Indian Dynasties*, Mumbai: Baratiya Vidya Bhavan Press, 2007.
8. Dharma Mittra, *Asanas: 608 Yoga Postures*, California: New World Library Press, 2003.
9. H. C. Raychaudhuri, *Political History of Ancient India*, Calcutta: University of Calcutta Press, 1972.
10. Satyananda Saraswati, *Asana Pranayama Mudra Bandha*, Munger: Yoga Publications Trust, 2008.
11. Judith Sankaranarayan, *Many Voices, One Song*, Delhi: Radha Soami Satsang Beas, 2013.
12. G. R. Sharma, *Excavations at Kausambi (1949-50)*, Memoirs of the Archaeological Survey of India, No. 74, Delhi: 1969. Reprinted, 1980.
13. R. Thapar, *Ashoka and the Decline of the Mauryas*, New Delhi: Oxford University Press, 2001.
14. W. W. Tarn, *Greeks in Bactria and India*, Cambridge: Cambridge University Press, 1951.
15. V. Trenckner ed. *Milindapanha,* London, 1880.

www.ingramcontent.com/pod-product-compliance
Lightning Source LLC
Chambersburg PA
CBHW030655230426
43665CB00011B/1108